Cooking Book

Indian Spice Trade

AN ANGLO-ASIAN CULINARY EXPERIENCE

Ismat Amin

AuthorHouse™ UK
1663 Liberty Drive
Bloomington, IN 47403 USA
www.authorhouse.co.uk
UK TFN: 0800 0148641 (Toll Free inside the UK)
UK Local: 02036 956322 (+44 20 3695 6322 from outside the UK)

Because of the dynamic nature of the Internet, any web addresses or links contained in this book may have changed since publication and may no longer be valid. The views expressed in this work are solely those of the author and do not necessarily reflect the views of the publisher, and the publisher hereby disclaims any responsibility for them.

Any people depicted in stock imagery provided by Getty Images are models, and such images are being used for illustrative purposes only. Certain stock imagery © Getty Images.

All illustrations and interior photos are by the author

This book is printed on acid-free paper.

ISBN: 978-1-6655-8008-3 (sc)
ISBN: 978-1-6655-8007-6 (e)

Print information available on the last page.

Published by AuthorHouse 01/28/2021

authorHOUSE®

Table of Contents

Vegetables, Chutneys, Sauces and Dressings

Meat 31

Fish 46

Pizzas and Pasta

Breads, Naans and Parathas

Desserts and Confectionary 68

Drinks 80

Introduction

I decided to write this book as I thought in Britain,where I live,and other parts of the world where many other Asians live, there is a mixture of European and Indo-Asian culture. So today in Britain there is Anglo-Asian cuisine, a mixture of Indian and European cuisine which is favoured by not only second generation Asians but also some first generation Asians.

Asians also change their tastes in food the longer they live abroad. So it was with my mother who came to Britain in the late Sixties with her children.Her cooking has changed from traditional Bengali to Anglo-Asian. So in our houshold our food range from rice dishes,many different curries and bhajis to lasagne, roast dinners to French dishes like Chowder.

Someone had said about my mother's cooking, 'Apa, your food isn't exactly Bengali. It's more Anglo'.
And right she is,so I was inspired to write this book.

The 'Cooking Book: Indian Spice Trade' is full of dishes that I cook and my mother cooks and we have had many glittering parties of these food-Anglo-Asian cuisine.

I was taught baking and English cooking by Mrs. Thomas, my Domestic Science teacher who taught me the basics of English cooking.My mother taught me Bengali cooking though some I picked up myself.

We also had a neighbour, two sisters Miss Smewing and Christine who made many cakes and pastry food who are a big influence on my cooking.

I hope you enjoy my recipes and dont labour over each dish.

Bon Appetit!

Ismat Amin

Snacks and Eggs

Vegetable Samosa

This is made using shortcrust pastry or ready made samosa pastry widely available in most supermarkets.

Ingredients for the pastry:

200g/8oz plain flour
Pinch of salt
40g/2oz butter or margarine
Water

Method:

In a bowl rub the fat lightly into the flour until mixture resembles fine breadcrumbs. Add 3-4 tbsp of the water into the mixture. Knead it until it is a dough. Add more water if necessary, or more flour if too doughy and sticky. Knead the dough lightly until firm and smooth. Do not overhandle the dough.
Set aside.

Ingredients for the filling:

½ packet of mixed vegetable (frozen or fresh).Usually
*   diced carrots, peas and chopped potatoes are used).*
2 -3 tbsp of vegetable oil if frying
1 tsp of turmeric
1 tsp of paprika
1 tsp cumin
½ tsp of salt

Method:

Divide the dough into rounds, make flat discs, roll into rounds, about 10 cm in diameter, then cut into half moons or semicircles.

Put the oil in a shallow frying pan, heat then put the vegetables with the spices and salt fry until tender. Set aside.

Put about 1 tbsp of the vegetable mixture in the centre of the half moon shapes. Brush the sides with a little milk and fold and seal the ends. Do this on a floured surface as it becomes sticky. Shallow fry the samosas in vegetable oil or bake in the oven in 190 degrees centigrade until golden brown about 15 mins. Turn over the samosas once.

Dry on a kitchen paper if frying them. Cool on a wire rack if baking them.

Serve with Coriander chutney. (Look under Chutneys for the recipe) or tomato sauce.

Makes 15-20
Variety-mince lamb or beef with peas or chicken and potato.

Folow the recipe above for the mince meat and peas except cook the sliced onions until glazed before cooking the peas and meat.

Again for the chicken and potato fry the sliced onions before cooking the chicken and diced potato

Crescent Pittha
(Pooli Pittha)

Ingredients:

For the pastry

120g/4 oz of plain flour
20g/1 oz of margarine
4 -5 tbsp of hot water to bind
Oil for frying

For the filling

40-60g/2-3 oz of coconut
40g/2 oz of sugar

Method:

Rub the margarine into the flour then add the hot water mix and knead until a soft dough. On a floured surface roll the dough and make rounds, 10cm in diameter.

In a pan place the coconut and sugar. Heat until a sticky mixture. Either place in a pittha maker (you can get in a Bangladeshi store), with the coconut mixture inside or fold in half and seal the sides with milk. You can pinch the sides or twist the sides. Deep fry the pittha until golden brown.

Serve hot or cold.

Serves 10-12

For a savoury version use ricotta cheese for filling.

Onion Bhaji (Fulori)

Ingredients:

1 onion sliced
3 tbsp or Garam flour or 40g/2oz of red lentils
1 tsp of turmeric
1 tsp of paprika
½ tsp of salt
½ fistful of fresh coriander
1 green chilli chopped
1 dsp of water
4 tbsp of vegetable oil

Method:

If using red lentils, soak in a bowl of water for ½ to 1 hour,then blend in a blender to a paste.In a bowl mix all the ingredients until stiff mixture. Add more flour or blended lentil if necessarry.

Heat the oil in a frying pan and spoon the mixture in a ball or you can flatten it if you like. Fry until dark brown on one side then turn over and fry again until crispy.

Serve hot or cold with tomato sauce, sweet and sour sauce or Coriander chutney (See Chutneys section for this recipe).

Serves 4

Tempura or Vegetable in Batter

Ingredients:

3-4 spinach leaves/1 paprika sliced
  or ½ an aubergine sliced
½ tsp turmeric
½ tsp of paprika spice
1 tsp of salt
20-40g/1-2oz of plain flour
½ cup of milk
3-4 tbsp of oil

Method:

Wash the vegetables.

On a plate put the spices and salt and mix and coat the vegetables in it.

Then make the batter with the flour and milk by mixing and beating it with a fork until a runny mixture. Dip the vegetables in the batter until coated and fry in the oil until golden brown on both sides.

Serve hot as a snack.

Serves 2-3

Bombay Toast

Ingredients:

1 egg beaten
1 slice of bread
1-2 tsp of sugar
Oil /margarine for frying

Method:

Mix the sugar in the egg and dip the bread in it until it has soaked both sides.

In a saucepan heat the oil and fry the soaked bread.

Serve hot or cold as a snack.

Serves 1

Variety- omit the sugar and add seasoning. I invented this version when I was living and studying in Dhaka in the early Eghties so I have dubbed it Dhaka Toast.

Chotpoti or Chickpea Curry

Ingredients:

1 small can of chickpeas or 80-120g/3-4 oz of fresh chickpeas lentil soaked in water overnight
½ medium sized sliced onion
750ml (1 ¼ pints) of water, you can use the water from the can or from the soaked chickpeas
1 tsp salt
2 tbsp of ghee or oil
1 tsp of turmeric
1 tsp of paprika
1 green chilli chopped fistful of fresh coriander (for garnish and flavouring)
1 medium sized chopped potato
1 tomato chopped
1 tsp of tamarind available in most supermarkets. If using fresh tamarind saok in boiling water before separating from the seed and using it as a flavouring
1 boiled egg chopped(for garnish)
½ packet ready salted crisps,crumbled (for garnish)

Method:

Fry the onion until glazed. Add the chickpeas, then the spices and salt and fry for 2-3 mins. Then add the chopped tomato, potato and chilli. Fry for another 1min. Add the water and bring to boil. Add the tamarind and ½ the coriander. When the water has evaporated away the chickpeas are cooked.

Cool and put in a glass bowl.

Garnish with the chopped boiled egg, fresh coriander and crumbled crisps.

Serve immediately.

Serves 4

On a plate sprinkle the breadcrumbs.You can make fresh breadcrumbs with pieces of bread in a blender. Dip the patties in the beaten egg and then cover with breadcrumbs. Fry in a shallow pan with the oil until golden on both sides.

Serve hot or cold as a starter or snack with Coriander or Mango Chutney(see Chutneys section for the recipe)

Serves 3-4

Potato or Aloo Chop

Ingredients:

3-4 New potatoes
2-3 tbsp of breadcrumbs
½ tsp of turmeric
½ tsp of paprika
½ tsp of salt
1 green chilli chopped
1 shallot or ½ onion chopped
1 boiled egg chopped
1 egg beaten
2-3 tbsp of oil

Method:

Boil the potatoes in a pan of water. Mash them with a masher and fork.Add the spices,salt, onion and chilli. Mix with a fork. Make little oval patties about 2 cm in diameter. Make an indentation in the middle and put a little of the chopped boiled egg and then close the indentation. Follow this until you have used up the mash and the egg.

Bubble

Ingredients:

3-4 New potatoes
2-3 leafy cabbage chopped
Seasoning
1 egg beaten
2-3 tbs of vegetable oil

Method:

Boil the potatoes with the cabbage. When cooked mash them and add seasoning. Make patties about 3cm in diameter. Dip them in the beaten egg and fry in the oil in a frying pan.

Serve hot as a snack with brown or tomato sauce.

Serves2-3

Smoked Salmon Tapas

I had this at the Marriott in Brussels in 2006.

Ingredients:

2-3 slivers of smoked salmon
1-2 tbs mayonaise
Seasoning
A packet of Dorittos/a tube of Pringles

Method:

Cut the smoked salmon into small pieces. Place the mayonaise in it. Season.

Serve with the Dorittos. Good for parties.

Serves 2-3

Egg Fried Noodles

Ingredients:

½ packet of dried or fresh noodles
1 tsp of soya sauce
¼ onion or 1 shallot chopped
580 ml/1 pint of water
1 egg beaten
1 cm root ginger grated
1 tsp of salt
1 tbsp of vegetable oil

Method:

Boil the noodles with the salt in a pan. Test with a knife if you can cut it. Drain and put aside.

Fry the onions in the oil in a shallow pan until softened. Place the ginger in the pan fry for a few seconds. Then place in the prawns or shrimps and fry until opaque in colour. Add the noodles in the pan and fry for a further 1 min. Then add the soya sauce in mix into the noodles. Finally add the beaten egg and fry until the egg has cooked.

Serve immediately.

Serves 2

Mixed Vegetable Pouches

Ingredients:

1 packet of filo pastrry
2 carrots diced
3-4 tbsp of peas
½ onion sliced
Seasoning
Olive oil for frying

Method:

Cut two sheets of filo pastry into 17cm rounds either with a cutter or an upside down cup.

Fry the mixed vegetables (you can use frozen) in the oil and onions until tender.

Place 1 tbsp of mixed vegetables in th centre of the rounds. Brush the edges with water or milk,twist the tops into pouches. Brush the outside with milk and place in the centre of the oven at 190 degrees centigrade and bake for 10 mins or until golden brown.

Prawn Mayonaise Tartlets

Ingredients:

Short crust pastry from the Samosa recipe.
20-40g/2-3 oz of frozen shrimps or fresh
  prawns peeled,washed and chopped.
2-3 tbsp of mayonaise
Seasoning

Method:

Make the shortcrust pastry and cut into 7.5 cm rounds. Place into tartlet cases. Bake blind until slightly brown. Cool on a wire rack.

Cook the prawns either in a microwave oven or steam with the seasoning until opaque or pink in colour. Drain and mix with the mayonaise and fill the tartlets.

Serve cold.

Variety- Chicken mayonaise canapes/tartlets

Substitute the prawns with seasoned grilled or boiled shredded chicken

Rosemary,Tomato and Cheese Canapes

Ingredients:

5 tomatoes chopped
2 tsp of olive oil
1 tsp of honey
Seasoning
40g/2 oz of crumbly cheese
2-3 olives pitted and chopped
A few rosemary leaves to garnish
1 box of Ritz biscuits

Method:

Arrange 10 biscuits on a platter. Mix the tomatoes,olive oil,honey,cheese and olives. Place on top of the biscuits and garnish with the rosemary leaves.

Serve cold.

Serves 10

Coconut Prawn Canapes

Ingredients:

10 raw tiger prawns
1 tsp of lemon grass paste or 1 stalk

1 shallot or half a onion chopped
1 cm of fresh ginger grated
1 clove garlic chopped
Pinch of ground coriander
Pinch or a few thread of saffron
1 tsp of oil
150ml/¼ pint of coconut milk
Seasoning

Method:

Peel the prawns and discard the tails. In a bowl place the first 8 ingredients and marinade. Cover and refrigerate for an hour. Place the prawn mixture in a pan with the coconut milk and seasoning and heat until the prawns become pink.

Arrange in Chinese soup spoons.

Serve warm.

Serves 10

Egg Dopiza

Ingredients:

4 hard boiled eggs
½ an onion sliced
1 tsp of salt
1 tsp of turmeric
1 tsp of paprika
300ml/½ pint of water
1 tbsp of vegetable oil

Method:

In a frying pan heat the oil.

Sear the eggs 4 times all around the egg then fry them in the oil until brown. Add the onions and fry until soft. Add the spices and salt and then the water. Simmer until the sauce thickens.

Serve hot with paratha (See Breads section for this recipe).

Serves 4

Sweet and Sour Poached Egg Curry

Ingredients:

4 eggs
1 onion sliced
1 tbsp of tamarind paste
2 tsp of sugar
Salt to taste
300ml/½ pint of water
1 tbsp of vegetable oil

Method:

Heat the oil in a frying pan and then add the onions and fry until soften. Place the tamarind sauce, sugar and water and simmer for 1 min. Then crack the eggs unbroken into the pan. Cover and cook until the eggs are soft boiled. Add salt to taste.

Serve immediately with white boiled rice.

Serves 4

Souffle Omlette

Ingredients:

2 eggs separated
Seasoning
2 tbsp of water
20g/1 oz of butter/margarine

Method:

Whisk the egg yolks until creamy add the seasoning and water and whisk again.Whisk the egg whites until stiff. Fold into the yolks using a metal spoon a few times

Place a little butter or margarine in a pan and coat it,then place the egg mixture in it,cover and cook over moderate heat until risen. Brown it under a hot grill. With a knife loosen the sides and tip onto a plate and put 1 tsp of jam preferably apricot,fold and dust with icing sugar with a sieve and serve.

Serve hot as a snack .

Serves 1

Spinach and Cream Fritata

Ingredients:

2 tbsp of vegetable oil
1 garlic clove crushed or 1 tsp of garlic salt
    (if using the latter do not add salt)
225g/12oz of spinach
Seasoning
6 eggs beaten
2 tbsp of fresh or clotted cream/creme fraiche
80g/3oz of cheddar cheese

Method:

Fry the garlic in the oil until brown. Then add the spinach.Season. Let the spinach wilt. Add the beaten eggs. Let the mixture cook until risen then transfer to a hot grill until the top is golden.

Alternatively before cooking the egg mixture you can transfer into a greased baking tin and bake in the oven for 15 mins. at 180 degrees centigrade.

Serves in wedges, hot or cold at a party.

Serves 4

Cheese and Onion Fritata

Follow the above recipe except substitute the spinach with 1 chopped onion and 60g/3oz of cheddar. cheese.

Soups

Mixed Vegetable Soup

Ingredients:

40-60g/2-3 oz of either frozen mixed vegetable or 1
   carrot peeled and sliced,some peas and sweetcorn
1 vegetable or chicken stock cube
300-500ml/1- ½ pint of water
1 tsp of cornflour
Season to taste

Method:

Wash the vegetables and place in a pan with the water,
crumble the stock cube . Bring to boil. Simmer with
the cornflour until water has reduced by a ¼, season
to taste.

Serve with crusty bread and Wocester Sauce

Serves 2-3.

Cream of Broccoli Soup

Ingredients:

1 broccoli cut into florets
Seasoning
20g/1 oz of butter
150ml/¼ pint milk
A dash of cream/evaporated milk

Method:

Boil the broccoli in a pan of water. When cooked,
test with a knife, drain the florets.Place the milk and
butter in the pan, blitz in a blender. Check there are
no broccoli bits.Take back to the stove and add the
cream. Adjust seasoning if neccesary.

Garnish with a sprig of mint or parsley.

Serve hot with crusty or sliced bread.

Serves 2-3

Chicken Soup

Follow the above recipe except with washed and
shredded chicken. After adding the cornflour add
a beated egg.

Serve either with Wocester sauce or soya sauce

Pumpkin or Butternut Squash Soup

Ingredients:

1 butternut squash or small pumpkin
20g/1 oz of butter
60g/3 oz of sugar
1 tsp of paprika
A pinch of salt
300ml/½ pint of water
A pinch of salt
Balsamic vinegar
A dash of cream/evaporated milk

Method:

Peel the butternut squash with a peeler or sharp knife. Scoop the seeds and fibres with a spoon.Cut into small pieces.Place in a pan with the water,spice,salt and sugar.Cook until the squash is soft and can be cut with a knife.Blitz in a blender.Check for bits. Place back on the stove, add the cream and reduce until a thick consistency.

When serving place a swirl of the balsamic vinegar.

Serve hot with crusty bread.

Serves 3-4

Tomato Soup

Ingredients:

4 -6 tomatoes
20g/1 oz sugar
Seasoning
150ml/¼ pint water
A dash of cream /evaporated milk
Chopped basil

Method:

Boil the tomatoes in the water. When cooked blitz in a blender and sieve. Place back on the stove, add the sugar,seasoning and the basil. Simmer until thick consistency. Pour the cream in the soup.

Serve hot with crusty or sliced bread.

Garnish with sprig of parsley.

Serves 3-4

Lemon Grass Soup

Ingredients:

2 onioins
225g/8 oz leeks
1 stalk of lemon grass/2-3 tbsp of lemon grass paste

80g/3 oz potatoes
37g/1.5 oz of butter/margarine
500 ml/ 1/8 pints of chicken/veg. stock
150 ml/ ¼ pint milk
75ml/ ¼ pint crème fraiche
Seasoning
Chives/spring onions to garnish

Method:

Peel and slice the onions.Peel and dice the potatoes. Slice the leeks.Slice the lemon grass.

Melt the butter in a saucepan,add the onions and leeks.Stir and place in 3 tbs of water. Cover and simmer for 10 mins. until soft.

Place in the potatoes,stock,milk and lemon grass. Cover and simmer for 20 mins until the potatoes are soft.

Place in a blender and blitz until smooth. Sieve if desired.

Season to taste.

Garnish with the chives or julien of spring onions.

Serve hot with prepared bread and butter sandwiches,crust cut off and cut into tiny squares or triangles.

Serves 3

Vegetables, Chutneys, Sauces and Dressings

Avacado with Prawn in Seafood Sauce

Ingredients:

4 avacados
120g/4oz of frozen shrimps
3-4 tbsp of Seafood sauce
Seasoning

Method:

Halve and stone the avacados. Wash the shrimps under cold running water until defrosted. Place in a bowl and add the seafood sauce and seasoning. Place the shrimps with the sauce in the cavity of the avacados.

Serve cold and as a starter.

Serves 4

Fried Mixed Vegetables (Bhaji)

Ingredients:

120g/4oz of fresh or frozen mixed vegetables
  or you can use a combination of both
½ tsp of turmeric
½ tsp of paprika
Salt ot taste
3 tbsp of vegetable oil

Method:

Chop and wash the fresh vegetables.

Fry the fresh vegetables in the oil in a shallow frying pan or wok for 5mins. Then add the frozen vegetables. Fry again for 1 min. Add the spices and salt. Cover and cook in low heat until the vegetbles are soft. You can test with a knife if the vegetables cut easily. You can put a little water and steam the vegetables until cooked.

Serve hot as an accompaniment with a main dish.

Serves 4

Fried okra/potol (Eastern vegetables like okra and potol found in most Asian groceries)

Follow the recipe above. Stalk the okra and chop them and cut the potol lenghtwise. Fry these, omit the water,do not steam.

Fried Aubergines

Ingredients:

1 medium sized aubergine
1 tsp of turmeric
1 tsp of paprika
1 tsp of salt
3 tbsp of vegetable oil

Method:

Wash the aubergine. Stalk and slice it. On a plate mix the spices and salt then coat the aubergine slices with them on both sides.

Fry in a shallow pan with the oil. If you cannot fit all the slices at once fry in batches. Turn over the aubergines once browned. Cook the other side also until brown.

Serve immediately as an accompaniment with a main dish and boiled white rice.

Serves 4

Aubergines Mash

Ingredients:

1 medium sized aubergine
½ an onion sliced
1 tsp of English or Dijon mustard. You
   can also use 2 tsp of mustard oil.
Salt to taste

Method:

Either half the aubergine lenghtwise and grill until the flesh is soft or cooked. You can also place the aubergine whole on a gas fire stove and cook until the the peel is dark and wrinkled. Transfer into a bowl and when sligltly cooled peel the aubergine or scoop with a dessert spoon if grilled, into a bowl.

Mash the aubergine with a fork, add the onions,salt and mustard.

Serve hot or cold with boiled white rice.

Serves 4

Mash Potatoes with Onions and Mustard

Ingredients:

5 New potaoes or 1 King Edward
½ onion sliced
1 tsp of Dijon/English mustard. You can
   also use 1 tbsp of mustard oil
Salt to taste

Method:

Boil the potatoes in a pan of water. You can also steam it in the microwave covered for 5-7 mins.
If using King Edward peel them when cool. You don't have to peel New Potatoes. Place in a bowl and chop with a knife,then mash with a fork. For a finer mash with no lumps use a masher.

Add the onions in the mash with the mustard. Mix with a fork. Put salt to taste.

Serve cold or hot as an accompaniment.

Serves 3-4.
Variety- you can make this with fried browned onions and red chillis in ghee or butter omitting the mustard.

Fried Potatoes/Sauted Potatoes

Ingredients:

2-3 New potatoes
½ tsp of paprika
Salt to taste
2-3 tbsp of vegetable oil

Method:

Slice the potatoes in fine chips or discs. Heat the oil in a frying pan. Place the potatoes with the paprika and salt. Fry until crispy.

For Sauted potatoes (discs) just sprinkle with salt when frying.

Serve immediately and as an accompaniment.

Serves 2-3

Baked Aubergine with Eggs

Ingredients:

1 aubergine
3-4 tbsp of vegetable oil
salt
200g/7oz of cheddar cheese
4 tbsp of tomato puree or tinned tomato puree
3 hard boiled eggs
1 egg beaten
4 tbsp of grated cheese

Method:

If using Spanish aubergines slice and sprinkle the salt on both sides and put on a colander with a weight to extract the bitter juices for 15 mins. and then wash. If using Asian aubergines this is not necessary.

Fry the aubergines in the oil until golden brown on both sides.

Slice the cheese and the boiled eggs.

In an oven proof dish put half the tomato puree in the bottom. Put a layer of aubergines,then the sliced cheese dipped in the beaten egg and then the boiled eggs. Repeat the process until all the aubergines,cheese and eggs are finished. Put rest of the tomato puree on top and top with the grated cheese. Bake in a oven at 200 degrees centigrade for 15 mins.

Serve immediately.

Serves 2-3.

Marrow Curry
with Shrimps

Ingredients:

1 marrow
40g/2oz of frozen shrimps
1 tsp of turmeric
1 tsp of paprika
1 fresh red chill chopped
1 onion sliced
3-4 tbsp of vegetable oil
1 tsp salt

Method:

Peel the marrow with a sharp knife or peeler. Cut in half lengthways and scoop out the seeds with a spoon. Then dice the marrow into small cubes.

In a saucepan heat the oil and then place the onions until softened then add the marrow, the spices and salt and again fry for a few mins., then add the shrimps. Cover and cook over low heat until the marrow is soft.

Serve hot as a side dish with white boiled rice.

Serves 4

Pumpkin Curry
with Shrimps

Follow above recipe except substitute marrow with pumpkin or butternut squash.

Serve as an accompaniment with white boiled rice.

Serve cold or hot and serves 4-6.

Crispy Seaweed

Ingredients:

220-750g /1/2-1 lb of spring greens-spinach, spring onions, lotus leaves
Oil for frying
1 ½ tsp of sugar
Salt to taste

Method:

Wash the greens and shred them and leave to dry for 30mins.

In a wok or deep fat fryer heat the oil until hot or sizzling and fry the greens until crisp. Remove with a slotted spoon and drain on a kitchen towel. Sprinkle with the salt.

Serve as an accompaniment.

Serve hot and serves 6-8 .

Waldorf Salad

Ingredients:

1 apple
4 celery stalks
4 tbsp of mayonaise or fromage frais
A few lettuce leaves
40g / 2oz of walnuts
1 lemon quarterd

Method:

Core but don't peel the apple then dice.Slice the celery. Mix the apple pieces, celery and the mayonaise or fromage frais.Then mix the lettuce leaves. Mix the walnuts (but leave some for garnish) and the lemon juice.

Garnish with the remaining walnuts.

Serves 3-4

Middle Eastern Pepper Salad

Ingredients:

4 long green peppers (from a Turkish shop)
3 dsp of natural yoghurt
Seasoning

Method:

Wash the peppers and slice lengthways.You can deseed if you like. Be careful they are quite hot. Place in a long dish and then put the yoghurt,seasoning and mix. Refrigerate until chilled.

Serve cold with Biryani or Honey roast chicken(see Rice and Meat section respectively).

Serves 4

Chutneys, Sauces and Dressings

Mango Chutney

Ingredients:

820g/4lb of ripe mango,peeled,stoned and sliced
2 onions chopped
600ml/1 pint of vinegar
240g/12 oz of demerara sugar
1 tbsp of ground ginger
3 garlic cloves crushed
1 tbsp of nutmeg
½ tsp of salt

Method:

Place all the ingredients in a pan, bring to boil, then simmer gently uncovered stirring occasionally until a thick consistency. Cool.

Sterilise a jam jar/jars, including the lid and then place the chutney in the jar.Close the lid tightly and place in the fridge.

Apple Chutney

Ingredients:

280g/3 lb of cooking apples
280g/3 lb of onions chopped

1.5l/2 ½ pints of vinegar
440g/1 lb sultanas
Grated rind and juice of 2 lemons or limes
660g/1 ½ lb of sugar
600ml/1 pint of vinegar

Method:

Follow the method from the above recipe.

Mango Pickle

Ingredients:

2.2kg/5lb of mangoes
Salt to taste
60g/3 ½ oz of fennel seeds
20g/1 ½ oz of chilli powder
1 onion sliced
20g/1 ½ oz of turmeric
A few dried chillis
600ml/1 pint of mustard oil

Rinse the mangoes,do not peel them.Then stone them and cut into small pieces. Place all the ingredients except the mangoes in a bowl and mix well. Then place the mangoes in the mixture until coated in the mixture.

Sterilise the necessary jars and place the mixture in it with some of the oil floating on top. Shut the lid tightly. Either refrigerate or put it in a sunny window ledge for the pickle to mature.

Olive Pickle

Ingredients:

20 green olives or Jalpai (Bengali olives, slighlty larger)
1 tsp of mustard seeds
1 tsp of cumin seeds or powder
½ tsp of chilli powder
½ of salt
3-4 tbsp of olive oil
100ml/1/3 cup of vinegar

Method:

Dry roast the mustard seeds,cumin seeds, add the chill powder. Once the seeds start to pop add the salt.Add the olive oil in a pan and salt. Fry for a min. then add the vinegar and simmer for 15 mins. Add the olives and mix.

When cool place the pickle in sterilised jar/jars, store either in a fridge or a sunny window ledge. This will preserve the pickle and enhance the flavour.

Lemon Pickle

Ingredients:

880g/2 lb lemons
30g/1 ½ oz of cumin seeds
200ml/8 fl oz of sesame oil or just vegetable oil
40g/2 oz of sugar
2 tbsp of ground ginger
1 tbsp of ground cardamom/cinnamon
1 tbsp of whole cloves
1tbsp of pepper
2-3 bay leaves
Salt to taste

Method:

Dry roast the cumin seeds until dark brown. Then grind them.Mix the cumin seeds with the rest of the spices.

Rinse the lemons and cut them into slices longitudinally.

Heat the oil in a pan, add the lemons and spices and fry for 5 mins.

Place in sterilised jar/jars. Cool and either put in the fridge or a sunny window ledge.

Coriander Chutney

Ingredients:

20g/1 oz of fresh coriander leaves
1-2 tsp of sugar
1-2 green chillis sliced
150ml/¼ pint of water

Method:

Place all the ingredients in a blender and blitz.

Raita

Ingredients:

½ cucumber diced
¼ carton of natural yoghurt
Salt to taste
½ tsp of ground cumin

Method:

Place all the ingredients in a bowl and mix.

Mint Sauce

Ingredients:

20g/1 oz of peppermint leaves
50ml/2 fl oz of vinegar

Method:

Place the ingredients in a blender and blitz.

Cranberry Sauce

Ingredients:

220g/8 oz of cranberries
220g/8 oz of sugar
300ml/½ pint of water

Method:

Place the cranberries in a pan with the water and bring to boil. Simmer until the berries have burst. Add the sugar and cook gently. Cool.

Oil Dressing:

This is just 2 tbs of vegetable oil with seasoning and mix with the salad.

French Dressing

This is equal proportion of oil to vinegar or lemon juice. Marinade the oil and vinegar or lemon juice for 5 mins. with 1tsp of sugar. Mix into the salad.

Yoghurt Dressing

Put one 1tbsp of natural yoghurt with 1tsp of ground cumin and mix into the salad.This is an Eastern dressing suitable for curries.

Vinegarette

Place one tsp of Dijon or grainy mustard to 4 dsp of vinegar and place in a small jar or locktite tupaware and shake.

Hoisin Sauce

Put equal quantities of soya sauce and honey and mix.

Rice Dishes

Chicken Biryani

Ingredients:

4-6 chicken thighs or drumsticks
160g/6 oz of basmati rice
1 onion sliced
1 tsp of turmeric
1 tsp of ground coriander
1 tsp of ground cumin
1 tsp of salt
2-3 dried red chillies
1cm of fresh ginger grated
2-3 tbsp of ghee or clarified butter
300ml/½ pint of water

Method:

Skin and wash the thighs or drumsticks.

Wash the rice either in a pan or bowl twice or three times and throw away the water.

In a medium sized pan heat the ghee and then fry the onions until soft. Then place the chicken in the pan with the onions fry until opaque. Then place the rice in the pan and fry for 3 mins. Place all the spices in the pan with the ginger and salt and fry using a toss and turn method until all the ingredients are covered with the spices. Then place the water in the pan until the chicken and rice is immersed in the water. Bring the pan to boil then simmer until the water has been absorbed. The rice may burn at the bottom you can place an atomiser on the bottom of the pan or stir it with a metal spoon so the rice doesn't stick to the bottom.

Serve hot as a main dish with salad,curry,kebab,fish cakes (tikka).

Serves 4-6

Pilau Rice

Ingredients:

1 onion sliced
100g/4 oz of basmati rice
2-3 tbsp of ghee or clarified butter
A pinch of salt
2-3 threads of saffron or food colouring
300ml/½ pint of water
20g/1oz of sultanas
Crispy onions or Beresta to garnish

Method:

Fry the onions in the ghee until softened. Then fry the washed rice for a few mins.Then place the salt in the pan and toss and turn for another min. Then place the water in the pan. Bring to boil and then simmer. Put in the sultanas at this point. When all the water has been absorbed put in the saffron threads or orange food colouring.The saffron threads have to be absorbed in a bowl of hot water until they have been dissolved. When the rice is multicoloured or jewelled then take off the cooker and put on a platter.

Garnish with Beresta or crispy onions. Look in the Beresta recipe below.

Serve hot as a main dish with Tikka and Chicken korma (See Meat section).

Serves 4

Beresta

Slice shallotts or onions very finely with a sharp knife. Then fry over a low heat in ghee until golden brown and crispy.

Prawn Biryani

Ingredients:

20-30g/2-3 oz of prawns or shrimps
80-1200g/3-4 oz of basmati rice
1 onion sliced
20g/1 oz of mixed fruits or raisins
1 tsp of cumin
1 tsp of ground coriander
1 tsp of turmeric
1 tsp of salt
20g/1 oz of Beresta
2-3 tbsp of ghee or clarified butter
300ml/½ pint of water

Method:

Fry the onions in the ghee until soft, then place the washed rice in the pan and fry for 1 min., then place all the spices, salt in and stir.

Head the prawns and peel the shells and place in the pan. Fry for a min. Place the water in the pan and bring to boil then simmer until the water has been absorbed. Place the mixed fruits in the rice and cook for a few mins. Test the rice if it is soft.

Garnish with Beresta.

Serve hot with salad or can be eaten with chutney.

Serves 3-4

Vegetable Biryani

Ingredients:

Mixed vegetable frozen or fresh
120g/4 oz of basmati rice
2-3 tbsp of ghee or clarified butter
1 onion sliced
300g/½ pint of water
1 tsp of turmeric
1 tsp of paprika
1 tsp of coriander
1cm root ginger

Method:

Fry the onion in the ghee, then add the washed rice. Fry them for a further 1 min., then add the the vegetables and fry again for a few mins. Add the spices and herb until coated in the rice and vegetables.

Then place the water in the pan and boil covered. After the rice and vegetable comes to boil lower the heat and simmer until the water has been absorbed. You can put a atomiser under the pan to stop the rice and vegetables from burning or stir it with a metal spoon.

Serve immediately as a main dish.

Serve 4

Couscous Biryani

Follow the above recipe except substitute the rice for couscous. Couscous is cooked by placing boiling hot water until the the couscous has expanded and then cooked like Biryani.

Serve immediately and as main dish.

Serves 4

Sushi

Ingredients:

20-40g/1-2 oz of Sushi rice (this is available in most Chinese groceries. However you can use the normal rice but when boiling do not throw away the starch),
1 sheet of Nori (again available in Chinese or Japanese groceries. Again if you can't get this you can substitute with leafy cabbage or spinach)

6-7 shrimps
1 sliver of smoked salmon or fresh salmon
2-3 slices of cucumber
Some cured ginger(again available in Japanese groceries. If you can't get this you can use fresh ginger sliced)
Some wasabi or green mustard
Some dark soya sauce

Method:

Cook the rice. When cooked spread it thinly on the Nori.If using cabbage or spinach steam it in a Chinese steamer for a few minutes to soften it. Make sure the spinach doesn't wilt. Roll the Nori into a sausage. Wait a few minutes for the rice to cool and the steam to absorb into the Nori. Then cut the Nori into 2.5cm pieces.

Meanwhile marinade the fresh salmon if using this in lemon juice or vinegar for 10-15 mins. Cut the salmon/smoked salmon into small pieces.

Dice the cucumber. Place one piece of salmon, one shrimp on each Sushi, then place the diced cucumber on top of this.When serving place soya sauce, wasabi and slivers of ginger on three little dishes to be eaten with the Sushis.

Serve as a snack with Japanese green tea or Jasmine tea.

Serves 2

Kicheri

This is served on a rainy day in Bangladesh but can be eaten on any day.

Ingredients:

40g/2 oz of long grain rice
40g/2oz of red lentil
1 tsp of Dijon or English Mustard.
    You can use mustard oil.
½ a sliced onion
Salt to taste
1 tsp of turmeric
1 tsp of paprika
300ml/½ of pint of water

Method:

Wash the rice and lentil in a pan of water and strain the water. Put the rest of the ingredients in the pan and mix. Then place the water in the pan and boil covered. Then simmer until the water is absorbed.

Serve immediately. This can be served with Mustard fish or Fried aubergines. (See Fish and Vegetable section respectively)

You can put mixed vegetable in the rice and lentil.

Chicken Risotto

Ingredients:

1.1kg/2 ½ lb chicken
1 onion quartered
1 carrot sliced

1 stick celery sliced
Seasoning
5 tbs of oil
400g/14oz of risotto rice or long grain rice
300g/½ pint of water

Method:

Remove the skin from the chicken and trim the fat. Cut it into pieces,off the bone.Put the bones into the rissoto for flavouring.

Heat the oil in a pan. Then add the onion,carrots and celery. Then the chicken and fry until brown.Ladle the water bit by bit.Bring the chicken to simmering point.Then add the rice and use up the rest of the water as previously until the rice absorbs all the water and is cooked. Remove the bones.

Serve immediately.

Serves 3-4

Egg Fried Rice

Ingredients:

4 tbsp of oil
250g/4oz of long grain rice
6 spring onions chopped/onions
300ml/½ pint of water
2 tbs of soya sauce
Peas (optional)

Method:

Heat the oil in a wok or large frying pan.

Wash the rice and place in the frying pan or wok and cook for 5 mins.add the spring onions and stir well. Pour in the water, cover,bring to boil and then simmer for 10 mins. Toss and turn the rice occasionally.

Serve immediately as a main dish or with a side dish.

Serves 4-6

You can cook this with left over rice without cooking the rice.

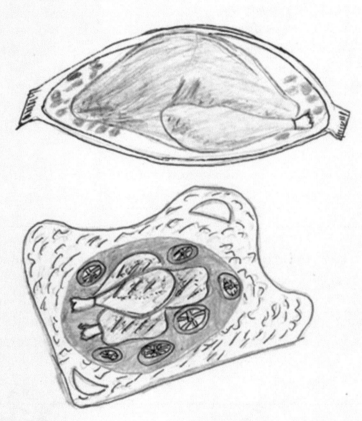

Meat

Chicken Korma

Ingredients:

1 chicken jointed or 6 drumsticks/thighs
20-30g/2-3 oz of cream or fresh coconut grated
1 cinnamon stick or bark
2-3 cinnamon pods or 1 cinnamon stick
2 bay leaves
150ml/¼ pint of milk/single cream or 1 can of coconut
   milk (if using this you don't have to use the coconut)
1 onion sliced
2-3 tbsp of cooking oil

Method:

Skin the chicken or drumsticks/thighs. Trim the fat. Wash it under cold water. Joint the chicken into small pieces.

Fry the onion in the oil until softened, then fry the chicken until the flesh is opaque. Place the herb in the pan and toss and turn until it is fragrant. Place the coconut and milk/cream in the pan. Bring to boil and then lower the heat and simmer until the liquid has reduced or thickened. When the chicken is soft, test with a knife, the korma is cooked.

Serve hot on a special occasion as a main dish with Pilau rice the (See Rice section).

Serves 4

Chicken Curry

Ingredients:

4-5 drumsticks/thighs skinned
1 cinnamon bark/stick
1 bay leaf
2-3 cinnamon pods
1 tsp of turmeric
1 tsp of paprika
1 onion sliced
½ tsp of salt
2-3 tbsp of vegetable oil
300ml/½ pint of water

Method:

Wash the chicken and trim the fat. Sear it with a knife.

Fry the onion until softened or glazed. Place the chicken in the pan with the oil and fry until opaque. Place the herbs and stir until fragrant. Place the spices, salt and coat evenly over the chicken. Pour the water into the pan and bring to boil and then simmer over low heat until the chicken is soft or the liquid is reduced and thickened.

Serve hot with either white boiled rice or naan bread.

Serves 4

Grilled Chicken with Peppers

Ingredients:

4-6 Chicken drumsticks/thighs skinned and trimmed
1 pepper sliced
1 onion quartered
1 tsp of turmeric
1 tsp of paprika
½ tsp of salt
1 tbsp of natural yoghurt
2 tbsp of vegetable oil

Method:

Wash the chicken and place in a grill pan. Place all the rest of the ingredients in a grill pan. Mix thoroughly with your hand or a spoon. Place under a hot grill until the chicken and vegetables are browned. Turn the chicken over once.

Serve immediately with toasted naan bread (see Bread section for this recipe).

Serves 4

For the Gravy

1 tbsp of flour
Seasoning
Melted butter/margarine/dripping

Method:

Wash the chicken inside and out. Season it on the outside. Brush it with the oil or smear it with butter. Make the stuffing according to the instruction on the packet. Stuff the inside of the chicken with it.

Place it in a large baking tray and bake in 200 degrees centigrade oven for half an hour or until golden brown basting it with the oil or melted butter now and then. Test it with a skewer if it is completely cooked inside. If it comes out clean it is cooked.

With the juices of the chicken put 1 tbsp of flour and put on the stove bring to simmer. Season and sieve and serve the gravy in a gravy boat.

Serve hot with roast potatoes,boiled vegetables and Yorkshire pudding. With the left over chicken you can make sandwiches served with Apple chutney (see Chutneys for recipe).

Serves 4-6

Roast Chicken with Gravy

Ingredients:

1 oven ready chicken
Seasoning
1tbsp oil/1 oz of butter
Sage and onion stuffing (packet)

Chicken in Pitta Bread

Ingredients:

4 pitta breads
4 fillets of chicken
1 tsp of coriander
1 tsp of grated ginger or powder ginger

2-3 tbsp of olive oil
½ tsp of salt

Method:

Cut the pitta breads in half and make pouches.

Wash and cut the chicken in small pieces. Marinade it in the rest of the ingredients for 15 mins. Grill under a hot grill until the chicken is brown. Place in the pouches.

Serve immediately for light lunch with Bio Yoghurt and Houmus mixed together.

Serves 4

Chicken Terrine

Ingredients:

4 chicken fillets or chicken off the bone
6 baby carrots
4 runner beans
1 egg beaten
2 tsp of tarragon
Seasoning
¼ cucumber diced
1 tomato diced or
150ml/¼ pint of passata
Sprigs of parsley to garnish

Method:

Wash the chicken and mince it with a mincer. Mix it with the egg and 1tsp of tarragon and seasoning.Layer a loaf tin with the mixture then put baby carrots on top. Then put another layer of the mixture then put

the runner beans on top. Put the rest of mixture on top and place in a ban marie (a tray of water) and bake in the oven for 30-45 mins. Test with a knife when cooked. With a knife loosen it from the tin and tip upside down on a platter.

Serve cold. When sliced you should be able to see the carrots and beans in the terrine. Serve with a chopped tomato and cucumber salsa or a passata and tarragon sauce, decorating the terrine in the corner with sprigs of parsley.Suitable for picnics.

Serves 4

Chicken Meatball Curry

Ingredients:

120-60g/4-6 oz of mince chicken
2 onion sliced
1 tsp of turmeric
1 tsp of paprika
½ tsp of salt
20-40g/1-2 oz of fresh chopped coriander
2-3 tbsp of vegetable oil
20g/1oz of cream coconut
300ml/½ pint of water

Method:

In a bowl mix 1 onion, the spices,salt and coriander. Make into small balls 2.5 cm in diameter.Fry in the oil in a pan until browned.Place the other onion in and fry until glazed. Place the coconut cream and water and bring to boil. Then simmer until the liquid has reduced and the chicken balls are cooked. Test with a skewer.

Serve hot with paratha or naan bread and salad (see Bread section).

For -variety use lamb mince instead of chicken mince.

Serves 4

Chicken/Lamb Liver Pate

Ingredients:

450g /1lb of chicken/lamb livers
50g / 2 oz of butter/margarine
1 onion chopped
1 garlic clove crushed
75ml or 5 tbsp of single cream or evaporated milk
15ml or 1 tsp of tomato puree
Seasoning
Parsley to garnish

Method:

Wash the livers and cut into pieces. Melt the butter/margarine in a pan add the onion and fry until soft. Add the livers and cook for 5 mins. Cool the livers and onion and then add the cream or milk, tomato puree and season.

Puree the mixture in a blender then place in a dish, cover and chill.

When serving garnish with parsley.

Serve on Melba or French Toast.

Serves 4

Chicken and Cucumber Mousse

Ingredients:

1.4kg/3lb of chicken
1 carrot peeled and sliced
1 onion chopped
1 tsp of tarragon
Seasoning
1 cucumber
2 tbsp of gelatine or 1-2oz/20-40g of China grass
20g/1oz of butter
2 tbsp of flour
2 tbsp of lemon juice
142 ml / 5 fl oz of whipping cream/evaporated milk
1 egg white
Fresh tarragon sprigs to garnish

Method:

Wash and skin the chicken. Put into a pan with the onion, carrot, herbs and seasoning into a pan with enough water to cover and bring to boil until chicken is tender. Take out the chicken pieces. Cool the chicken and cut into small pieces and mince.

Reduce the cooking liquid to 400ml then sieve and put aside.

Finely dice ¾ of the cucumber. Soak the gelatine/china grass in a small bowl. Place the bowl over a pan of simmering water and stir until dissolved.

Melt the butter/margarine in a pan and stir in the flour and cook for 1 min., stirring. Remove from the heat and stir in the stock. Cook the stock until boiling and the sauce thickens. Remove from the heat and stir in the gelatine and then the chicken. When cold add the diced cucumber, lemon juice and seasoning.

Whisk the egg white and mix with the milk. Add to the chicken mixture.

Place into a deep glass dish,cover and refrigerate to set.Decorate with the remainder cucumber slices on a plate and sprigs of tarragon and place the bowl on it.

Serve as a Summer dish.

Serves 6

Murgh Mussalam

You can also use poussin/baby chicken for this dish. This is Middle Eastern dish but the Asians have adopted it.
Ingredients:

2 onions sliced
2 cloves of garlic crushed
5cm of root ginger peeled and grated.You
  can use a grinder for this as well.
½ carton of of natural yoghurt
1 tsp of garam masala
1 oven ready chicken
125g /4 oz of long grain rice
3 tbsp of butter or ghee
1 tsp of chilli powder
50g /2oz peeled almonds cut into halves

30 ml /12 floz of water
3-4 tbsp of sugar

Method:

Put the onions,garlic,sugar and the yoghurt into a blender or food processor and work into a paste. Stir in the garam masala and add salt to taste.

Prick the chicken all over with a fork and rub the blended mixture and let it marinade for 1 hr.

Wash the rice and heat 1 tbsp of the butter/ghee in a pan and fry the rice for 3 mins.,stirring. Add the chilli powder and almonds. Add salt to taste. Pour in 15ml/6 fl oz of water and bring to boil and then simmer covered until the water is absorbed.Set aside.

Put the remaining ghee/butter into a deep pan and melt it and then put in the chicken with the marinade and bring to simmer.Cook for an hour covered,turning the chicken over. Add salt to taste. When chicken is cooked, stuff it with the cooked rice.

Serve hot as a main dish. You can either carve the chicken or in true Eastern style tear the meat with your hands.

Serves 4-6.

Thai Green Curry

For this recipe you need Thai green paste.

Ingredients:

For the Paste

1 lemon grass stalk finely chopped or 2 tsp of paste
40g/2 oz of coriander leaves
2 tsp of coriander seeds
1 tsp of lime rind grated
½ tsp of salt

For the Dish

2 shallots or 1 onion chopped 2 tbsp of groundnut oil
2.5cm of fresh ginger peeled and crushed
½ can of coconut milk
1 tsp of Nam pla/Shrimp paste
1 tsp of sugar
5 small green chillis
2 lime leaves, or dried kaffir leaves crushed
2 garlic cloves sliced and fried
2-4 chicken thighs or drumsticks

Method:

Put the first 5 ingredients in a food processor or blender and blend to fine paste.

Heat the oil in a wok and stir fry the ginger, shallots over low heat for 3 mins. Add the Thai green paste and fry for 2 mins. Add the chicken and fry for 3 mins. Stir in the coconut milk and bring to boil. Simmer for 10 mins. until the chicken has cooked and the sauce has thickened. Stir in the Nam pla or Shrimp paste, sugar, kaffir leaves and chillis. Cook for a further 5 mins. Add salt to taste.

Garnish with the fried garlic.

Serve immediately with rice noodles.

Serves 4

Chicken Satay

Ingredients:

900g/2lb of chicken off the bone cut into 2.5cm thin pieces

For the Marinade

2 tbsp of vegetable oil
2 tbsp of soya sauce
2 tbsp of tamarind paste
1 lemon grass stalk chopped or 1 tsp of paste
2 garlic cloves crushed
1 tsp of ground cumin
1 tsp of ground coriander
1 tbsp of lime juice
1 tsp of brown sugar

For the Peanut Sauce

2 tbsp of peanut butter
200ml/7floz of coconut cream
1 tbsp of Nam Pla/Shrimp Paste
1 tbsp of brown sugar

Method:

Blend all the ingredients of the marinade in a food processor and place in a bowl and add the chicken and toss to coat. Cover and refrigerate for about an hour.

To make the sauce put all the ingredients in a pan and heat gently until smooth. Keep warm.

Thread the chicken into skewers and grill for 3-5 mins., turning once until the chicken is cooked. Serve with the sauce.

Serve immediately as a starter or snack.

Serves 8

Honey Roast Chicken

I first had this dish in Brussels. It is a Middle Eastern dish.

Ingredients:

1 poussin or baby chicken skinned
2 dsp of honey
2 dsp of oil preferably olive oil
1 tsp of cumin
1 tsp of peri peri medium to hot sauce
1 tsp of salt
4 cinnamon or cardamom pods
2 cinnamon sticks or barks

Method:

Wash the chicken and leave to dry.

Crush the cinnamon pods and break the cinnamon barks to let out the flavour and fragrance.

Put all the ingredients in a large bowl and mix. Make sure you mix all the ingredients inside and outside of the chicken. Cover and refrigerate for ½ an hour to marinade.

After ½ an hour put the chicken with the spices and sauce on a baking tray, cover with foil and bake in a oven at 200 degrees centrigrade for about 45 mins. or until it is golden. Test with a skewer if it is cooked. Make sure there is no red flesh.

In a rottisserie cook the chicken for the same amount of time.

Garnish with Beresta or crispy fried onions (see above for recipe).

Serve hot with Biryani.

Serves 3-4.

Barbecue Chicken

Ingredients:

4 chicken drumsticks or thighs skinned and trimmed
2 onions sliced
1 tsp of turmeric
1 tsp of paprika
1 tsp of salt
2 tbsp of natural yoghurt

Method:

Wash the chicken and put 2-3 three sears on them. In a large bowl place all the ingredients and mix well. Cover and refrigerate for ½ an hour to marinade.

Cook on a barbecue until char browned turning several times with tongs. Check if it is completely cooked.

Serve hot with toasted naan bread and a salad (see above and Bread section).

Serves 4

Rogan Gosht

Ingredients:

4 tbsp of oil
2 onions chopped
750g /1 ½ lb lamb/mutton cubed
1 carton of natural yoghurt
2 cloves of garlic
1 inch piece of root ginger
2 green chillies
1 tbsp of coriander seeds
1 tsp of mint leaves
1 tsp of coriander leaves
1 tsp of cumin seeds
6 cloves
6 cardamoms
1 cinnamon stick or bark
Salt to taste
120g/4 oz of almond flakes

Method:

Heat the oil in a pan, add the onion and fry until golden.

After washing the lamb pieces place in the pan .Add ½ of the carton of yoghurt, stir, cover bring to boil and simmer for 20 min.

Place the garlic, ginger, chillies, coriander, cumin, mint and 3 tbsp of the remaning yoghurt in an electric blender or food processor and blend to a paste. Place the paste into the pan, add the cardamoms, cloves and cinnamon stick, stir. Add salt to taste. Continue simmering for a further 30 mins. Add the almonds and cook until the lamb is tender.

If you wish to cook this dish in a Pressure Cooker in half the time you may do so without compromising on the flavour.

Serve immediately with Pilau rice/naan bread or Chicken biryani as a main (see Pilau rice in Rice section for recipe).

Serves 4

Lamb Curry

Ingredients:

680g/1 ½ lb of pieces lamb on the bone (if you
ask the butcher they will do this for you)
1cm of root ginger
Salt to taste
1 tsp of cumin powder or seeds crushed
1 tsp of turmeric powder
1 tsp of paprika
1 green chilli cut in half
1 pint of water
3 tbsp of vegetable oil
2 onion sliced

Method:

Wash the lamb. Heat the oil in a saucepan and fry the onions until softened.

Crush the ginger in a grinder and add to the pan, then the spices and then the chilli. Add the lamb and fry until light brown in colour. Add salt to taste, then the water and bring to boil and then simmer until tender for 45 mins. -1 hr. Test with a knife if cooked.

Serve hot with boiled white rice/naan bread/rooti and a side dish of fried vegetables (see Bread and Vegetable section).

Serves 4

mince. Fry until brown in colour. Add the turmeric, paprika and cumin and ginger and fry for 2 mins. Add the salt and tomato puree and the peas. Add the water and bring to boil and then simmer until the mince is cooked. Just before taking it off the cooker add the coriander leaves. Taste to see if cooked.

Serve immediately with white boiled rice/naan bread (see Bread and Vegetable section respectively).

Serves 4

Lamb Mince with Peas

Ingredients:

680g/1 ½ lb of mince lamb (the
  butcher does this for you)
2.5cm root ginger crushed
2-3 cinnamon pods
1 cinnamon bark
1 bay leaf crumpled
40g/2 oz frozen or fresh peas
2 tsp of tomato puree or 1 tomato chopped
1 fistful of washed fresh coriander leaves
1 tsp of turmeric
1tsp of paprika
1 tsp of cumin powder
1 green chilli halved
Salt to taste
300ml/½ pint of water
1 onion sliced
4 tbsp of vegetable oil

Method:

Wash the mince.

In a pan heat the oil and fry the onion until softened. Add the cinnamon pods, bark, bay leaf and then the

Lamb Tikka or Kebabs

Ingredients:

440g/1 lb of lamb mince
1 onion sliced
1 tsp pf turmeric
1 tsp of paprika
1 tsp of salt
20g/1 oz of coriander leaves chopped
2 green chillis sliced
1 tbsp of vegetable oil
1 egg beaten

Method:

With a hand blender or food processor mince the lamb mince to a paste.

In a bowl place the mince,onions,coriander leaves,chillis,spices and salt. Mix with your hand and make into about 5cm diameter pattis or tikkas. Dip each tikka in the egg and fry in a shallow pan with the oil. When golden brown turn and repeat the process.

Serve hot or cold as a starter or accompaniment with Pilau rice and Chicken korma (see Rice and this section respectively).

Serves 4

Grilled Lamb Chops with Parsley Butter

Ingredients:

1 bunch of parsley
2 cloves of garlic
1 shallot or ½ an onion chopped
1 tsp of salt
5 tbsp of unsalted butter or margarine
Juice of 1 lemon
4 lamb chops
50ml/2 fl oz of double or single cream

Method:

Peel the garlic and put in a blender with the onion,parsley,lemon juice and butter.

Trim the lamb chops and boil them.Take out of the water and arrange them on a roasting tin. Grill them with the cream. Grill until tender, test with a skewer. Spoon the parsley butter on top and grill until the butter melts.

Serve hot as a main meal.

Serves 4

Grilled Italian Lamb with Rosemary Oil

Ingredients:

2 lamb fillets trimmed
4 garlic cloves crushed
2 onions quartered
4 tbsp of oil seasoned with rosemary
Seasoning

Method:

Make a small incision with a sharp knife on the fillets and insert the garlic. Heat the griddle pan put the fillets in the pan and cook, turning once until charred.After 30 mins. add the onions. In a mortar and pestel or grinder blend the rosemary, oil and seasoning. Spoon over the fillets.

Serve hot with boiled pasta topped with cheese.

Serves 4

Crown Roast of Lamb

Ingredients:

2 best necks of lamb each with cutlet
20 g/1oz of butter or margarine
1 onion or 2 shallots chopped
1 eating apple,peeled,cored and chopped
1 celery sliced
20g/1 oz of breadcrumbs
1 tsp of chopped peppermint or parsley

Juice of one lemon and rind
1 egg
Seasoning
2 tbsp of flour
400ml/¾ pint of stock
2 tbsp of oil/dripping

Method:

Melt butter in a saucepan and cook the onions, celery and apples until brown. Stir in the breadcrumbs, half the mint, lemon rind and juice, egg and seasoning. Allow to cool and fill the centre with the stuffing.

Place in a roasting tin and spoon over with the oil or dripping, cover with foil and roast at 180 degrees centigrade for 25 mins. Baste occasionally.

Take out of the oven, bend the joints inwards or tie them with a string to form a crown. Place on each joint a small rossette cover so you can eat with your fingers.

The Sauce

Drain of the fat from the tin. Cook for 2 mins. Stir in the mint/parsley, the flour and stock and boil for 2-3 mins. Stir continously and serve with the joint.

Serve hot with roast potatoes and boiled vegetables.

Serves 6

Stir Fried Orange Beef

Ingredients:

2 tbsp of sesame seed oil
2 tbsp of soya sauce ½ inch of root ginger

2 tbsp of corn flour
350 g/12 oz of rum (optional)
5 steaks cut into strips
1 dried red chilli
4 tbsp of vegetable oil
Pinch of salt
1 tangerine/ orange peel cut into strips

Method:

Combine half the sesame oil, soya sauce, ginger and cornflour, add the meat, toss until coated. Leave to marinade for 15 mins.

Heat the vegetable oil in a frying pan or wok and add the chilli and stir fry for 30 secs. Place the meat in the pan with the orange rind, salt, sugar and the rest of the soya sauce. Stir fry for 4 mins. Sprinkle the rest of the sesame oil on the beef.

Garnish with the orange slices.

Serve hot with Fried rice (see Rice section).

Serves 4

Salt Beef

Ingredients:

1 joint of beef
3-4 tbsp of salt
2-3 cinnamon pods
1-2 cinnamon sticks
1 small jar of horeseradish sauce
½ jar of mayonaise

Method:

Wash the joint of beef. Smear it with the salt and leave for 3-4 hrs.

Wash the salt off and immerse it in a large pot of water with the cinnamon pods and sticks. Boil for 2 hours. Check with a skewer.

Serve sliced. Mix the horseradish sauce and mayonaise and serve with the beef.

Serve cold as slices or use in sandwiches.

Serves 8

Duck in Pineapple

Ingredients:

1 whole duck
3 tbsp of oil
150ml/¼ pint of water
2 tbsp of white vinegar
2 tbsp of dry sherry (optional)
2 tbsp of soya sauce
¼ tsp of 5 spice powder
1 green chilli sliced
1 small ripe pineapple or small tin of pineapple
1 inch root ginger
1 clove garlic
3 tsp of cornflour

Place the duck in a wok with the oil and fry until opaque in colour. Put the rest of the ingredients except the pineapple, in the wok and simmer covered until tender.

Cut the top of the pineapple and peel the outer layer with a sharp knife. Either remove the eyes with a knife or do diagonal cuts across the pineapple's eyes until all the eyes are removed. Slice the pineapple into thin slices omitting the core as this is quite hard.

Remove the duck from the marinade and place in a fridge. When cool skim the fat. Slice the duck in strips and mix with the pineapple. Stir fry the duck with the pineaple for a few minutes.

Serve with Fried rice (see Rice section).

Serves 8

This is a Chinese version of the classic French dish Duck a l'orange.

Peking Duck

Ingredients:

1 whole duck
3 tbsp of oil
8 sprigs of spring onions
½ cucumber sliced into juliens
Hoisin sauce

For the pancakes:

4 oz of plain flour
A pinch of salt
2-3 tbsp of water
1 tbsp of oil

Method:

Wash and dry the duck. Place in a baking tray, smear with the oil and bake in 200 degrees centigrade for 45 mins. until brown. Test with a skewer when cooked.

For the pancakes mix the first three ingredients in a mixing bowl until a stiff dough. Add some more flour if the dough is sticky. Make little balls about 5cm in diameter and roll with a rolling pin until small pancakes. Dry fry the pancakes in a frying pan or pancake pan then coat each side with the oil. Put the pancakes in layers and steam in a steamer for 3 mins. The pancakes should separate.

Slice the duck in thin strips. Cut the sprigs of spring onions in 1cm strips.On each pancake place some of the duck, spring onions and julien of cucumbers and add a spoonful of the Hoisin sauce(see Sauces for this recipe above) and serve.

Serve hot at a party.

Serves 10

Duck in Coconut

Ingredients:

1 whole duck skinned and jointed
3 cardamom pods or cinnamon pods
3 bay leaves
3-4 tbsp of oil
1 can of coconut milk or 120g/4oz of cream coconut
1 tsp of turmeric
1 tsp of chilli powder
1 tsp of cumin

1 tsp of salt
1 onion chopped

Method:

Wash the duck.

Put the oil in a wok or karai and fry the cardamom and the bay leaves for a min. Then put the all spices and fry for a further 2-3 mins.

Place the duck in the karai and toss and turn until the duck is light brown in colour. Add the salt. Fry covered until the juices of the duck is given out in the pan for about 30 mins. Add the coocnut milk or the cream coconut mixed in a pint of water. Cook covered for an hour or until the duck is tender. Check with a knife or skewer.

For Bhuna duck sweat off all the juices.

Serve hot with Pilau rice or rice flour rooti (see Rice and Bread section respectively).

Serves 6

Tandoori Quail

Ingredients:

175 ml / ¼ pint of plain yoghurt
1 onion sliced
1 clove garlic crushed
1 inch of grated ginger
1 tbsp of garam masala
Juice of 1 lemon
4 quails
1 tbsp of melted butter or ghee

Method:

Wash the quails and skin them.

Mix the first five ingredients in a bowl and place the quails in it. Marinade the quail in the spices and herbs and lemon juice for 1 hour.

Thread the quails in skewers and place in the roasting tin for 10-15 mins. In the oven at 220 degrees centigrade, basting it in the melted butter at regular intervals. Turn the skewers once.

Serve hot with a salad in natural yoghurt dressing (see Dressings section for recipe) and white boiled rice or naan bread(see Bread section for recipe).

Serves 4

You can substitute woodpigeons for quails.

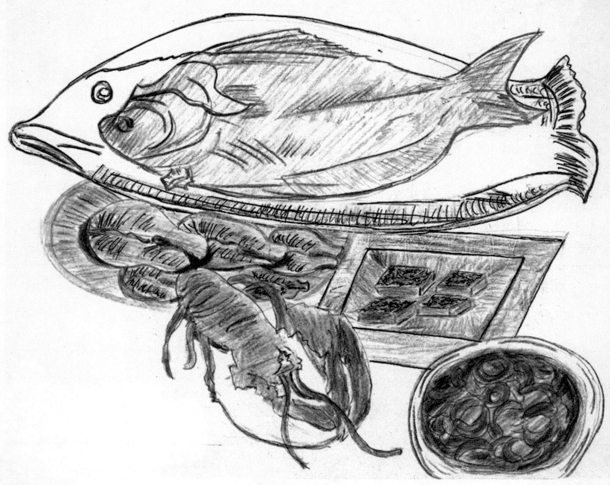

Fish

Baked Trout with Mustard Mash

Ingredients:

1 Rainbow trout,scaled and gutted
1 King Edward potato boiled and mashed
1 tsp of mustard or mustard powder
1 onion sliced
2 tsp of breadcrumbs
1 tsp of salt
2 tbsp of olive oil

Method:

Wash the trout.

Place the salt and 1 tbsp of oil in the inside.Place salt on the outside of the fish as well.

Mix the mustard and onions with the mash potato and season.

Stuff the inside of the fish with the mash and leave some for the topping. Sprinkle the top with the breadcrumbs.Drizzle the the top with the remaining oil and put in a hot oven at 200 degrees centigrade until golden brown.

Serve hot on its own or with a salad.

Serves 2

Fish in Hollandaise Sauce

Ingredients:

2 trout steaks(or any fish)
300ml/½ pint of milk
Seasoning

For the Hollaidaise Sauce

2 tbsp of vinegar
1 tbsp of water
2 egg yolks
220g/8 oz of butter/margarine
Seasoning

Method:

Place the trout steaks in a pan with the milk and seasoning. Poach until fish is cooked.

For the Hollandaise Sauce

Place the vinegar and water in a saucepan and boil until reduced by half. Cool.

Place the egg yolks and the vinegar liquid in a bowl over a pan of gently simmering water and whisk until the mixture is thick and fluffy.

Melt the margarine or butter and gradually add it to the eggs. If you have a food processor you can do this in it. Season. When it has a thick consistency the sauce is cooked.

Sieve the milk, if you like, from the poached fish and add to the sauce and pour over the fish.

Serve hot with mash potatoes or minted boiled Jersey potatoes.

Serves 2-4.

Steamed Japanese Trout

Ingredients:

1 Rainbow trout,scaled and gutted
2 tbsp of soya sauce
2.5cm root ginger, grated or grinded
2 tsp of vegetable oil
2 tbsp of rice vinegar
1 clove garlic crushed
Ground black pepper

Method:

Wash the fish.

Smear with the soya sauce, ginger, vinegar, garlic and pepper inside and outside of the fish.

Either place in a fish kettle or cut in half the fish and put in two layers of a Chinese bamboo steamer. Steam until the fish is cooked or soft. Check with a knife.

Serve hot with white boiled rice.

Serves 2

Salmon in Breadcrumbs

Ingredients:

Freshly ground pepper
4 salmon fillets /steaks with skin
120g/4 oz of breadcumbs
6 tbsp of chopped herbs fresh or dried
    like parsley or tarragon
¼ tsp of nutmeg
80g/3 oz of nuts
120g/4 oz of butter/margarine
1 tsp of salt
1 beaten egg
Garnish with fresh herb sprigs

Method:

Wash the fish and then sprinkle with salt and pepper on the skin of the fish.

Mix the breadcrumbs, herbs, and nutmeg together.

Chop the nuts and place in the mixture.

Melt the butter in a frying pan and stir the breadcrumb mixture into it.

Dip the salmon with the beaten egg and coat with the breadrumb mixture. Place in a oven at 200 degrees centigrade for 20 mins until the salmon is opaque and the crust is golden and crisp.

Transfer to individual plates and garnish with the herb.

Serve hot with a salad.

Serves 4

Traditional Fish Curry

Ingredients:

*Any English or Asian fish cut into
  steaks or pieces of fillets
1 onion sliced
1 green chilli chopped
1 tsp of salt
1 tsp of turmeric
1 tsp of paprika
1 fistful of coriander
3 tbsp of vegetable oil
300ml/½ pint of water*

Method:

Wash the fish.

Fry the fish and onions to seal the fish in a shallow pan. Add the chilli,spices and salt. Fry for 1 min. then add the water and coriander. Cook for 5-7 mins. until the fish is cooked.

Serve hot with white boiled riced and fried vegetables (see Vegetable section).

Serves 3-4.

Traditional Fried Fish (Fish Bhaji)

Ingredients:

*Any English or Asian fish cut into steaks or pieces
1 onion sliced*

*1 tsp of turmeric
1 tsp of paprika
1 tsp of salt
2-3 tbsp of vegetable oil
1 red pepper sliced (optional)*

Method:

Wash the fish.

Fry the onions until crisp and golden. Set aside.

Fry the fish to seal it, then add the spices and salt. Fry until the fish is crisp and brown. Sprinkle the fried onions on top.

Serve hot with Fish curry or as a starter (See above).

Serve 2-3

Hilsa Fish with Mustard Seed Oil

Ingredients:

*1 hilsa fish (available in Bengali grocer, you
  can use herring if you cannot get this fish)
2-3 table spoonfuls of mustard oil
1 oz of mustard seeds
1 tsp of turmeric
1 tsp of paprika
1 tsp of salt
1 onion sliced
150ml/¼ pint of water*

Method:

Wash, scale and gut the fish. Sometimes you can get the fish gutted. Cut off the head and tail. You can eat this and has a lot of flavour. Cut the fish into steaks.

Fry the onion in the oil until softened. Fry the steaks, head and tail to seal it. Then sprinkle the spice and salt on top of the fish. Gently stir the fish to coat in the spices and salt so as not to break it. Then sprinkle the mustard seeds and pour the water. Simmer for 10-15 mins. until fish is cooked.

Serve hot with Kicheri (See Rice section).

Serves 4

Rui Fish Balls

Ingredients:

1 rui fish (available in Bengali grocer) if you
    can't get this salmon is a good alternative.
1 onion chopped
1 tsp of paprika
1 tsp of turmeric
1 green chilli chopped
1 fistful of fresh coriander
6 tsp of vegetable oil

Method:

Wash and scale the fish. Head and tail the fish.

Fry the fish in a large saucepan with half the oil. When cooked take the flesh off the central bone. Check there are no small bones in the fish. Take the flesh off the head and tail.

In a bowl mix the fish with the rest of the ingredients. Form into small balls 2.5cm in diameter. Fry the balls in the remaining oil until golden.

Serve hot in a party or as a side dish with white boiled rice.

Serves 6-8.

Salmon Kedgeree

Ingredients:

2 salmon fillets
40g/2oz of peas
1 bunch of parsley chopped
2 tbsp of curry powder
1 tsp of salt
1 leek sliced
1 fish stock cube
2 poached eggs
300ml/½ pint of milk
120g/4 oz of rice
4 tbsp of vegetable oil

Method:

Poach the salmon in a pan with the milk.

Wash the leeks and in a pan fry them in the oil. Then place the parsley in the pan, then the rice and fry for 1 min. Then place the stock in the pan with the rice, parsley and leeks. At this point you can place the peas with the rest of the ingredients. Bring the rice to a boiling point, then simmer until all the stock has been absorbed.

Take the salmon out of the pan after it has been poached,flake it.

You can place some of the milk into the rice as it has a lot of the flavour. Sweat off the excess milk from the rice.

Mix the salmon and the rice.

Poach the eggs in a poacher or immerse in a pan of boiling water until soft boiled.Take out with a slotted spoon if the latter.

In a long dish or rice platter place the Kedgeree.

Garnish with the poached eggs.

Serve hot for breakfast or for lunch.

Serves 4

Salmon with Tomatoes and Coriander

Ingredients:

2 salmon fillets
2 tomatoes chopped
1 tsp of paprika
1 tsp of turmeric
1 tsp of salt
1 fistful of coriander
3 tbsp of vegetable of oil
1 onion sliced
300ml/½ pint of water

Method:

Wash the salmon fillets and cut them into pieces.

Fry the onions in the oil and the salmon pieces to seal it. Place the spices and salt in the pan. Just stir the fish without turning it over as the fish will break. This is to mix the spices evenly. Place the tomatoes in the pan and fry for a few mins. Pour the water into the pan, simmer until fish is opaque in colour. Then sprinkle the coriander on top.

Serve hot with white boiled rice.

Serves 3-4

Grilled Fish

Follow the recipe for Grilled chicken in the Meat section above,omitting the yoghurt. You can use fillets or steaks.

Serve warm and with a rice dish or eat on its own.

Serves 2

Salmon with White Foaming Grape Juice

Ingredients:

6 fillets of salmon
75ml/3 fl oz of water
75ml/3 fl oz of grape juice or white wine
20g/1 oz of butter
Seasoning

For the Sauce

125ml/5 fl oz of grape juice or white sparkling wine
300ml/1 pint of fish stock (fresh
   in a tub or from a cube)
2 tbsp of chopped basil/dried basil
450ml/15 fl oz double cream
Seasoning

Method:

To Cook the Sauce

Pour the grape juice and fish stock into a pan and place over heat.Once the sauce has reached boiling point place the basil leaves, boil for about 10 mins. or until the liquid is reduced to half. Pour in the double cream and whisk.Bring to boil until the sauce thickens. Season. Reserve aside.

To Cook the Salmon

Take a shallow baking tray and pour in the water and the grape juice, place the fillets in the tray with a knob of butter on each fillet, season. Cover the tray with foil and cook the fillets for 10 mins. in 200 degrees centigrade until opaque in colour. Check with a knife when cooked, that the inside is cooked.

Take each fillet and place on a plate and serve the sauce on top.

Serve hot for Christmas or New Year dinner.

Serves 6

Sea Bass with Cappuccino Sauce

Ingredients:

2 sea bass fillets
2-3 sprigs of dill
¼ pint of milk
1 small carton of single cream
1 egg beaten
Seasoning

Method:

In a fish kettle or steamer steam the fish with the seasoning until cooked.

In a pan pour the milk, cream and a egg. Heat gently and then whisk into a froth.

Serve the fish in deep bowls and pour the froth mixture on top.

Garnish with a sprig of dill.

Serve hot with minted boiled Jersey potatoes.

Serves 2

Gravalax

Ingredients:

4 slivers of smoked salmon
Seasoning
20g/1oz of chopped dill

For the Sauce

2-3 dsp of mayonaise
100ml/1/3 cup of dijon mustard/1 tsp of mustard powder
Seasoning

Method:

Marinade the salmon in the seasoning and dill. Cover and refrigerate for about 2 hours.

For the Sauce

Mix all the ingerdients together. Usually you can have this mixed with steamed fennel or without the fennel in a sandwich.

Serve cold, ideal for Summer lunches.

Serves 2-3

Salmon Mousse

Ingredients:

4 salmon fillets (frozen or fresh)
2-3 eggs beaten
½ tin of evaporated milk/1 medium
  size carton of single cream

Salt to taste
½ cucumber chopped, save the other half for garnish
300ml/½ pint of milk

Method:

Wash the salmon.

Poach the salmon fillets in the milk in a pan. When opaque in colour, drain the fish and flake and place in a food processor with the evaporated milk,eggs and salt.

Dice the cucumber and mix into the mixture with a spoon.

Grease a salmon mousse mould or a heat proof dish with depth. Put the salmon and cucumber mixture in it and place in a shallow baking tray with water and cook it as a ban marie. Bake in an oven at 200 degrees centigrade for half an hr. to 45 mins. When the mixture is set, test with a skewer it should come out clean when completely cooked. To get it out of the mould, loosen the salmon mousse with a knife, then soak in hot water and put it upside down on a plate, tap the base and the fish mixture should come out whole.

Garnish the top and around the salmon with the sliced cucumber. Refigerate.

Serve for lunch in the Summer or at parties.

Serves 5-6.

Baked Salmon

Ingredients:

1 whole salmon,gutted and scaled
4-5 carrots
1 whole cucumber
1 medium sized onion chopped
1 green chilli sliced
1 fistful of fresh coriander
1 tbsp of turmeric
1 tbsp of paprika
1 tbsp of cumin
1 tsp of salt
Some olive oil

Method:

Head and tail the fish and place the fish, with head and tail in a fish kettle.

Steam the fish whole as you'll need the central bone. Steam until the fish is tender. You can test it with a knife when cooked. The flesh will be soft and opaque.

Separate the fish from the central bone and put in a bowl. Reserve the central bone to rearrange the fish. Flake the fish and pick out the small bones with your hand.Mix the onions, chilli, coriander, spices and salt into the mixture.

Peel the carrots, wash and slice into discs. This will form the scales of the fish.

Place the central bone in a large baking tray and reconstuct the fish in a fish shape. Decorate with the carrots as scales. Put the head and tail next to the fish for baking as these can be eaten and you'll need them to reconstuct the fish when serving. Drizzle the fish with the olive oil.

Place in the middle rack of the oven and bake until golden brown or firm at 200 degrees centrigade.

When cooked lift the fish with a flat spoon or slide onto a large fish plate or platter. Reconstuct the head on top and tail at the bottom. Slice the cucumber and decorate around the plate.

Serve hot or cold with Potato salad or Hollandaise sauce (see previous recipe for the latter).

Serves 8-10.

Steamed Fish in Roux Sauce

Ingredients:

1 whole fish scaled and gutted or 4 fillets /steaks
Seasoning
1 tbsp of oil
1 Spanish onion
A bunch of sorrel leaves

For the Roux Sauce

40g/2 oz plain flour
1 knob of butter/margarine
Seasoning
300ml/½ pint of milk

Method:

Wash the fish and leave it to dry. Season the fish and smear the inside and outside with the oil.

Slice the onions and place inside the fish and on top.

Place the fish, onions and sorrel leaves on top of the fish, in a fish kettle or steamer. You can also use a metal colander. Steam for 15-20 mins. or until the fish is tender. Check with a knife. The fish should be opaque in colour. Lift the fish out and place in a platter with the onions.

For the Roux sauce put the fish water in a pan
In a frying pan fry the flour, then add the butter and seasoning. Pour the milk and stir with a fork until there is no lumps and is a smooth mixture. Boil until it is thick and creamy.

Pour the sauce in a gravy boat over the fish.

Serve hot with mash potatoes.

Serves 3-4

Prawn Curry in Coconut

Ingredients:

1 onion chopped
1 garlic clove chopped
2.5cm of ginger chopped
1 tsp of turmeric
1 dried red chilli or ¼ tsp of chilli powder
420g/1lb of prawns
¾ pint of coconut milk or cream
  coconut dissloved in milk
Juice of 1 lime
½ tsp of salt
Shredded coconut to garnish

Method:

Place the first 7 ingredients with the salt in a food processor and blend to a thick paste. Transfer the paste to a pan and fry gently for 5 mins, add the prawns and fry for a further few mins. Then pour in the coconut milk, stir it gently and bring to boil. Then

simmer for 10 mins. until the prawns are cooked. Don't overcook as the prawns will be rubbery.

Garnish with the coconut.

Serve hot with white boiled rice.

Serves 2-3

Lobster in Coconut

Ingredients:

2 lobsters, peeled and washed with the tentacles
Salt ot taste
½ onion sliced
1 tsp of turmeric
1 tsp of paprika
1 tin of coconut milk
3 tbsp of vegetable oil

Method:

Cut the lobster into 2.5cm pieces. In a saucepan fry the onions until soft, then place the lobster and tentacles in it. Add the spices, onions and salt in and fry for 1 min. Then pour the coconut milk in the pan and simmer gently until the lobster is pink in colour.

Serve hot with Pilau rice (See Rice section).

Serve 2-4

Lobster in Butter

Ingredients:

2 whole lobsters peeled and halved.
  Reserve the peel to serve.
120g/4 oz of butter
Salt to taste

Method:

Wash the lobsters.

In a baking tray place the lobsters with the butter on top and sprinkle with the salt. Grill under a hot grill until golden brown. Place the lobsters back in the peel.

Serve hot as a starter.

Serves 2

Lobster Thermidor

Ingredients:

2 whole lobsters peeled, with the tentacles
40g/2 oz of butter/margarine
1 onion choppd
2 tbsp of parsley/coriander/dill
1 tbsp of tarragon
4 tbsp of white wine or grape juice
½ of Bechamel sauce
3 tbsp of grated cheese
1 tsp of mustard
½ tsp of salt
½ tsp of paprika

For the Bechamel Sauce

½ pint of milk
½ onion sliced
½ celery chopped
½ carrot peeled and sliced
1 bay leaf
3 black peppercorns
20g/1 oz butter/margarine
20g/1 oz of flour
Seasoning
2 tbsp of single cream/evaporated milk

Method:

Remove the peel from the lobsters, wash them and cut into pieces.

Melt half the butter, add the the lobster, tentacles and onions. Fry for a few mins. Then add the spices,herbs and salt in and fry for few mins. Then add the mustard and wine and simmer for 5 mins. Place in a deep dish and set aside.

For the Bechamel Sauce

Place the milk, carrots, celery, bay leaf and peppercorns in bowl and set aside to infuse for about 15 mins.- ½ an hour.

Melt the rest of the butter in a pan, stir in the flour and fry over low heat for 1 min.

Strain the milk and stir into the flour.Bring to boil, stir until the sauce thickens. Season and stir in the cream/milk.

Place the mixture in a deep dish in the oven and place the grated cheese on top and brown under the grill.

Serve hot with crusty bread.

Serves 2-3

Chowder

Ingredients:

2 fillets of haddock
4 New potatoes diced
Salt to taste
1 tsp of freshly ground pepper
300ml/½ pint of milk
1 fish stock cube
1 tbsp of f;our
1 tbsp of chopped parsely
1 onion chopped
4 tbsp of vegetable oil
600ml/1 pint of water

Method:

Wash the fillets and cut into chunks.

In a big pan fry the onions in the oil until softened. Then add the salt and pepper. Then add the potatoes. Fry for few mins. Dissolve the fish stock cube in the water and pour into the pan. Simmer for 8 mins. until the potatoes are cooked.Then add the parsley and milk. Simmer for a few mins.

In a little milk mix the flour and and pour into the Chowder making sure it doesn't form lumps. Stir continously until the stock thickens.

Serve hot.

Serves 4

Moorighonta

This is a curry made with yellow lentil and the head of a fish. You can cook this with a Bengali fish available from a Bangladeshi grocer.
Ingredients:

1 whole fish head
75ml/½ cup of yellow lentil washed
1 tsp of turmeric
1 tsp paprika
1 tsp of salt
1 pint of water.
1 onion sliced
2 tbsp of vegetable oil
Some fresh coriander to garnish

Method:

Wash the fish head.

Fry the onion in the oil then the head, break into pieces when softened or cooked. Add the spices and salt, fry for a further few mins. Add the lentil and fry for 1 min. Then add the water and simmer until the fish head and lentil are cooked or about 10 mins.

Garnish with the coriander.

Serve hot with white boiled rice.

Serves 2-3.

Tuna/Salmon Fish Cakes

Ingredients:

1 tin of tuna or 2 tuna steaks
A pinch of salt
1 green chilli chopped
1 onion chopped
Some coriander leaves chopped
1 egg beaten/mashed potato to bind
Vegetable oil

Method:

Place all the ingredients in a bowl and mix. For the tuna steaks,steam until cooked in a microwave and place in a bowl. Make into patties about 5cm in a diameter and 1cm thick. If using mashed potato dip in a beaten egg before frying.

Fry in the oil in a shallow pan until both sides are golden.

Serve hot or cold as a snack or starter or side dish.Can be eaten with a Tomato and cucumber salad.

Serves 4

Tuna Sashimi

Ingredients:

Tuna steaks frozen or fresh
50ml/2 fl oz of vinegar
2 radishes
Some wasabi
Mint leaves to garnish
Some dark soya sauce

Method:

Marinade the tuna steaks in the vinegar for 15 mins. until the flesh turns opaque. Serve on a plate when marinated with the shredded radish .

Garnish with the mint leaves.

Eat with the wasabi and soya sauce.

Serve cold eat as a main meal with Japanese green tea or Sake.

Serves 3

Pizzas and Pasta

Vegetable and Chicken Pizza

Ingredients:

1 pizza base/flat bread
1 pepper sliced
1 onion sliced
2-3 baby corns
Seasoning
1 tbsp tomato puree
2-3 tbsp of olive oil
Cheddar/ mozarella cheese grated

Method:

You can make the pizza base by following a bread recipe(see in the Bread,Parathas and Naan recipes).

Spread the tomato puree on the pizza base.

Fry the vegetables in the olive oil until they have softened. Place on the pizza base,season and top with the cheese and bake in a oven 200 degrees centigrade.

Serve hot in wedges with a salad.

Serves 2-4

For Chicken pizza substitute the vegetables with cooked chicken pieces and sliced spring oinions.

For a Venetian pizza make the toppings with chopped onions,pitted black olives and currants. Omit the cheese.

Bruchetta with Pesto Sauce

Ingredients:

1 mini pitta bread/half a naan
1 tomato chopped
¼ onion chopped
1 tsp of Pesto sauce
2 tsp of olive oil
Seasoning

Method:

Mix the Pesto sauce with the olive oil.

On the pitta bread place the onions and tomato, season and drizzle with the Pesto sauce and olive oil. Grill under a hot grill until brown.

Serve hot as a snack or starter.

Variety -try with Red pesto sauce.

Serves 1

Pitta Bread with Creamed Mushrooms

Ingredients:

1 mini pitta bread/ ½ a naan
2-3 button mushrooms sliced
3-4 tbsp of evaporated milk/single cream
Seasoning
2-3 tbsp of vegetable oil

Method:

Toast the pitta bread/ ½ a naan.

Fry the mushrooms in the oil for a few mins.,season and pour in the cream,let it sizzle then pour over the pitta bread.

Serve hot as a snack or starter.

Serves 1

Ciabatta with Courgettes, Peppers and Onions

Ingredients:

1 Ciabatta bread split in half
¼ courgette sliced
2 slices of peppers
¼ onions chopped
1 tsp of olive oil

Method:

Place the vegetables and onions on the Ciabatta, drizzle with the olive oil. Grill until brown.

Serves hot as snack or light lunch.

Serves 1-2

Spaghetti Bolognaise

Ingredients:

20g/1 oz of butter/margarine
220g/8oz minced beef/lamb
1 onion chopped
1 carrot peeled and sliced
1 celery sliced
1 clove garlic chopped
1 bay leaf
1 tbsp of tomato puree
300ml/½ pint beef/chicken stock
Seasoning
450g/1.25lb spaghetti/pasta
Cheddar cheese grated

Method:

Wash the beef.

Heat the butter in a saucepan, add the beef and cook for 5 mins. until opaque in colour. Add the onion, carrot, celery and bay leaf. Stir and cook for 2 mins. Add the tomato puree, stock and seasoning. Bring to boil, then simmer uncovered for 45 mins.,stirring occasionally.

Cook the spaghetti in a saucepan with boiling water with some salt until cooked. You can cut the spaghetti or pasta with a knife easily when cooked. Drain and mix with the beef in the sauce, top with the cheese. Serve on a platter.

Serve hot.

Serves 4

Curried Chicken Lasagne

Ingredients:

4 drumsticks/thighs skinned and trimmed
6 lasagne sheets
40g/2 oz butter/margarine
2 tbsp of flour
1 tsp of turmeric
1 tsp of paprika
1 tsp of cumin
400ml/¾ pint of milk
20g/1 oz of dessicated or cream coconut
1 tbsp of fresh breadcrumbs
Seasoning

Method:

Remove the flesh from the chicken. You can cook the chicken with the bone as the bone has a lot of flavour.

For the Sauce

Melt butter in a saucepan, stir in the flour and the spices, seasoning and fry for a min., stir in the milk and bring to boil until the sauce thickens. Simmer for 5 mins, add the coconut.

For the Dish

Place some of the chicken in the base of a shallow dish, then arrange the lasagne sheets on top and pour some of the sauce. Do this until the sheets and the chicken is used up. Pour the rest of the sauce on top, then place the breadcrumbs on top. Bake in a oven 180 degrees centrigade until the topping is brown.

Serve hot.

Serves 4

Variety- you can make Lasagne Bolognaise which is delicious. I had this at the Crowne Plaza in Brussels in 2006. Follow the recipe for Spaghetti Bolognaise except substitute the spaghetti with lasagne sheets and do layering.

Pasta Veronese

Ingredients:

120g/4 oz of pasta
1 chopped tomato
1 tbsp of tomato puree
Seasoning
1 onion sliced
40g/2 oz of prawn peeled or shrimps
1 garlic clove crushed
½ carton of single cream/evaporated milk
¼ pint of water
20g/1 oz of cheddar/parmesan cheese grated
2 tbsp of olive oil

Method:

Fry the onions in the oil until softened. Add the tomatoes, garlic, and fry for a min. Then add the prawns.

Fry until the prawns are pink in colour.

Boil the pasta in salted boiling water until cooked. Check with a knife when it is cooked. Add the pasta to the pan with the prawns, then add the puree, stir until all the pasta is coated in the tomatoes,onions and the puree, pour in the cream and simmer for a few mins. Place in a deep dish and top with the cheese.

Serve hot.

Serves 3-4

Breads, Naans and Parathas

Pizza Base

Ingredients:

10g/½ oz of yeast
1 pinch of sugar
150ml/¼ pint of luke warm water
680g/1 ½ lb of white flour
2 tsp of salt
Knob of butter/margarine

Method:

Blend the yeast with the water and the sugar and place in a warm place for 15 mins. until frothy.

Mix the flour, salt in a bowl and rub in the butter. Make a hole in the centre and place the yeast in it. Stir.Work into a firm dough, mixing more flour if too sticky. Mix it until the dough doesn't stick to the sides. Place the dough on a floured surface and knead for 10 mins. until the dough is elastic and firm. Place back in the bowl, cover with a damp tea towel until the dough has doubled in size. Again knead the dough to burst the air bubbles. Roll into a round flat base and place on a greased roasting tin or baking sheet and bake in a hot oven of 230 degrees centrigrade for 30 mins. until it has risen or golden brown.

Serve cold as a pizza base.

Serves 4

Naan Bread

Ingredients:

10 oz/300g of plain flour
1 sachet of yeast
½ tsp of salt
1 ½ tsp of sugar
4 tbsp of milk
10g/1/2oz of melted butter/margarine
100 ml/ ¼ pint of water

Method:

Follow the pizza base recipe to make the dough. Knead until smooth. Roll onto a floured surface 0.5cm thick and 25cm in diameter round base. Place on a large baking sheet and grill on the uppermost shelf on the highest setting of your grill. Cook for 2-4 mins. until they are brown . Turn over and repeat the process.

Serve hot .

Serves 6

For variety-you can place a ½ oz of fresh coriander in the dough mix.

Peshwari Naan

Place 40g/2oz fresh or dessicated coconut and 20g/ 1 oz of white sugar in the dough mixture.

Traditional Paratha

Mogli Paratha

Follow the above recipe, instead of putting knobs of butter inside, brush with a beaten egg, fold into a square and then rolled out again, dip in rest of the beaten egg and fry as above.

Serve hot.

Serves 1

Ingredients:

120g/4 oz of plain flour
40g/2 oz of butter/margarine/ghee
1 knob of butter/margarine/ghee for frying
½ tsp of salt
¼ pint of warm water

Method:

Place the flour, salt and water in a bowl and mix with your hands to a dough. Add more flour if sticky. Roll onto a floured surface. Place little knobs of the butter all over the dough, fold the sides to make a small square about 7.5 cm long sides. Roll out again on a floured surface into the original size.

In a frying pan fry the paratha until brown, then place a knob of butter on the sides of the paratha until it melts and goes under the paratha. Fry for 1 min. or it is golden brown. Turn over and repeat the process.

Serve hot for breakfast with a curry or Vermecelli.

Serves 4

Rooti

Ingredients:

120g/4 oz of plain flour
½ tsp of salt
150ml/¼ pint of warm water

Method:

Place the flour and salt in a bowl. Place the water in it and mix into a dough with your hands adding more flour if sticky. Make into little rounds in the palm of your hands and on a floured surface roll out into round thin circles about 13.5cm in diameter. Fry on a tawa (a flat pan like the old griddle pan or a tortilla pan) until both sides are brown.

Serve hot or cold for breakfast or with evening meal.

For variety- use rice flour for Rice rootis.

Serves 6

Lichees

Ingredients:

180g/6 oz of self raising flour
40g/2 oz of butter or margarine
½ tsp of salt
¼ pint of water
½ pint of oil for deep frying

Method:

Place the first 4 ingredients in a bowl and mix with your hands into a dough. Roll out the dough on a floured surface. Either cut with a knife geometrical shapes or cut with a biscuit cutter. Fry in a deep pan with the oil until golden brown and has puffed up.

Serve hot with Egg halva (see Dessert section for this recipe) or a curry for breakfast.

Serves 4

Desserts and Confectionary

Roshmalai

Ingredients:

1 litre/1 ¾ pint full cream milk
Some lemon juice
680g/8 oz sugar
400ml/¾ pint of water
1 large tin of evaporated milk
4 cinnamon pods
2 tsp of chopped almonds
1 tbsp of plain flour

Method:

In a large pan boil the milk.Put enough lemon juice into the milk until it forms or separates from the liquid. Place the curd in a muslin cloth or a sheer material which will strain the liquid without the curd. Place on a plate and put a weight on it so the liquid will strain quickly. Take the curd out of the muslin and place in a bowl. Place the flour and curd in it and knead it to a smooth dough. Make little oblong rolls about 5cm long or flat ovals discs.

Boil the sugar and water in a pan,place the rolls in the syrup and boil for about 20-30 mins. Take the rolls out of the syrup with a slotted spoon and set aside. You can use the syrup for sweetening other desserts.

Simmer in a pan the evaporated milk with the cinnamon pods, add more milk if necessary. Then place the rolls in it, cool and refrigerate over night.

Serves 6-8.

Shondesh

Follow the above recipe for the curd. Place back on the stove after straining it. Add 4-5 oz of sugar, stir it until it is sticky. Put the same amount of cinnamon pods. Take it out of the pan and spread it on a platter. Cool and refrigerate.

When set cut into squares or diamonds.

You can also use clay moulds you can get in Bangladeshi departmental stores. Make sure you grease the moulds before placing the Shondesh in it.

Serves 8-10.

For variety-when cooking the curd add 2-3 oz of chopped pistachio. This is very famous in this country and will be green in colour and is Pishtacio halva. You can also add some green food colouring if isn't very green.

Sweet Yoghurt with Mollases

This is a very famous dish from Northern Bangladesh, Bogra
Ingredients:

1 medium size carton of natural yoghurt
80g/3 oz of mollases or muscavado sugar
1 large tin of evaporated milk

Method:

Put all the ingredients in a large heatproof decorative bowl and whisk.

Place in the centre of the oven and bake for about 3-4 hours on the lowest setting- 50 degrees centrigade until set. Cool and refrigerate.

Garnish with a sprig of mint.

Serve with a scoop.

Serves 6

For variety- you can make this without mollases but instead of evaporated milk and sugar use a small tin of condensed milk. This is a sharp taste but is very popular. You can make a fruit version by using a fruit yoghurt and serve with a tsp. of jam.

Rice Pudding

Ingredients:

40g/2 oz of rice pudding rice
850ml/1 ½ pint of water
20-40g/2-3 oz of sugar or sugar to taste

1 large tin of evaporated milk
300ml/½ pint of milk
4-5 cinnamon pods
2 cinnamon barks or sticks broken
1 bay leaf
20g/1 oz of sultanas
Chopped almonds to garnish

Method:

Wash the rice in a pan with water.

Boil it in the water in a pan. Simmer until the rice is cooked or soft or the water has been absorbed. Place the milk and evaporated milk, cinnamon pods, barks and bay leaf in the pan and simmer until half the liquid has evaporated away. Place sultanas in it and simmer for a few mins.

Place the Rice pudding in a large decorative bowl, garnish with the chopped almonds, cool and refigerate.

Serves 6-8

Ground Rice Pudding

Ingredients:

80g/3 oz of ground rice
Sugar to taste
600ml/1 pint of milk
2-3 dsp of Rose water
Sultanas to decorate

Method:

Place the ground rice, water and sugar in a pan. Boil until it is creamy. Stir so as there is no lumps. Place the Rose water in it and mix.

Place in a decorative bowl, decorate with the sultanas, cool and refigerate.

Serves 4-6

Semolina

Ingredients:

20g/1 oz of semolina
300ml/½ pint of milk
20g/1 oz of sugar or sugar to taste
1 knob of ghee/butter
2-3 cinnamon pods
1 bay leaf
1 cinnamon bark

Method:

Place all the first 4 ingredients in a pan and bring to boil or until becomes a sticky texture, Stir. Place the rest of the ingredients in the pan and mix. Check for lumps.

Place on a platter and garnish with chopped almonds. Cool and refrigerate.

Cut into diamonds.

Serves 6-8

Faluda

Ingredients:

1 medium size carton of crème fraiche
40g/2 oz of China grass (available in Indian groceries)/1 sachet of gelatine
20-40g/2-3 oz of sugar
2-3 drops of vanilla extract/rose water
300ml/½ pint of water

Method:

Place the crème fraiche in a shallow bowl.

Boil the China grass in a pan with water until it has all melted. Stir or whisk until there is no China grass visible. Place in the bowl of crème frache. Place also the sugar in the bowl. Whisk. Place the vanilla extract in the mixture and stir. Cool and refrigerate until set.

Serve in wedges.

Variety-you can use 1 can of coconut milk and 150ml/¼ pint of milk instead of crème fraiche.

Serves 4-6

Lentil Halva

Ingredients:

120g/4 oz of yellow
120g/4 oz of sugar
120g/4 oz of ghee/butter
400ml/¾ pint of water

4-6 cinnamon pods crushed
1 large can of evaporated milk
300ml/½ pint of milk
40g/2 oz of chopped nuts preferably almonds
Almond halves and sultanas to garnish

Method:

Wash the lentil in a pan and strain the water. Place more water in the pan and soak for 45 mins to 1 hr. Drain the water and place in a blender and blend to a paste.

Place in a pan with the sugar and ghee.Cook until it bubbles. Place the cinnamon pods in the pan. Stir continously, add the evaporated milk and the normal milk and mix. Cook for 10 mins. until the mixture is sticky. Add the chopped nuts, and stir.

Place on a platter, flatten into a smooth mixture and decorate with the almond halves and sultanas. Cool and refigerate.

Cut into squares or diamonds.

Serve with tea/coffee or as a snack.

Serves 10.

Variety- instead of lentil you can use butternut squash peeled, deseeded and chopped.

Baklava

This is traditionally a Middle Eastern recipe but has spread to the Medditeranean countries.

Ingredients:

220g/8 oz of chopped walnuts/ pichtachio/almonds
40g/2 oz of sugar
½ tsp of ground cinnamon powder
1 lb of filo pastry
140g/5 oz of melted butter
160g/6 oz of honey

Method:

Grease a roasting tin or baking sheet.

Mix the nuts, sugar and cinnamon in a bowl.

Halve each filo sheet. It doesn't matter if it breaks. Place it on a baking tin or sheet. Brush with the melted butter and scatter some of the nuts on it. Do this 5 times. Then bake in the oven for 20 mins. at 200 degrees centigrade until golden brown. Cool and drizzle with the honey.

Cut into squares or diamonds.

Serve cold with Middle Eastern Mint tea or Spice tea (look under Drinks for these recipes).

Serves 20

Variety -you can use chopped apples instead of the nuts.

Apple Crumble

Ingredients:

2 apples (any variety)
20g/1 oz sugar
120g/4 oz plain flour
40g/2 oz butter/margarine
1 tbsp of water
1 tsp of nutmeg

Method:

Peel, core and chop the apples. Sprinkle some lemon juice on them to prevent from browning. Set aside.

In a bowl rub the margarine and flour together until it resembles fine breadcrumbs. Place the sugar in the bowl and mix. Place the apples in a shallow oven proof dish and place the water in it and then top it with crumble mixture,making sure you cover all the apples. Finally sprinkle the nutmeg on top.

Bake in a oven at 190 degrees centigrade until golden brown.

Serve hot or cold with cream or evaporated milk.

Serves 4

Cauliflower Piash(pudding)

Ingredients:

1 medium sized cauliflower
120g/4 oz sugar or sugar to taste
4 cinnamon pods

1 cinnamon bark
600ml/1 pint of full cream milk
½ can of evaporated milk
40g/2 oz of ghee/butter

Method:

Cut the cauliflower into florets. Wash it.Just grate the top of the florets, being careful not to get any of the stems as the pudding will smell of the cauliflower.

In a pan melt the ghee and fry the grated cauliflower, add the sugar,spices and the two milks. Stir until reduced into a creamy sauce. Place in a decorative bowl,cool and refrigerate.

Serves 8-10

Variety- instead of cauliflower you can use grated marrow.

Egg Halva

Ingredients:

4 eggs beaten
4 cinnamons pods crushed
1 cinnamon bark
You can use vanilla extract intsted of the above 2 ingredients
½ tsp of orange food colouring /saffron
40g/2 oz of sugar or sugar to taste

Method:

Place the eggs in a pan and heat, whisking continously. Add the cinnamon pods, bark and the sugar. Whisk until it forms into small lumps or coagulates. Add the food colouring. Stir. Place on a platter .

Serve hot or cold with Lichees or paratha for breakfast (see Bread section).

Serves 4

Zabigloni

Ingrdients:

4 egg yolks
40g/2 oz sugar
150ml/¼ pint of milk
Crushed ameretti/cappuccino biscuits to garnish
Method:

In a pan of water place a heatproof bowl with the yolks and beat with a whisk.Heat and whisk continously making sure the egg yolks don't coagulate.Add the sugar and milk. Wait till it forms into a custard consistency.Remove and place either in wine glasses or tea cup and saucer.

Garnish with the amaretti or cappuccino biscuits. Cool and refigerate until set.

Serve cold or hot as a dessert.

Serves 3-4

Lime Cheesecake with Chocolate Leaves

Ingredients:

1 small box of full or half fat cream cheese
1 tub of mascarpone cheese
40g/2 oz of caster or normal sugar
Zest of one lime and its juice
1 bar of cooking chocolate
½ packet of digestive biscuits or any sweet biscuits
40-60g/3-4 oz of melted margarine or butter
Some rose leaves(for making the chocolate leaves)

Method:

In a bowl mix the the 2 cheeses, then place the sugar, the zest and the juice of the lime. Mix thoroughly.

In a plastic bag or tea towel break the biscuts until fine crumbs with a rolling pin.You can use a blender. Mix the melted butter with the crumbs and in a shallow dish,press the crumbs into a thin layer, then place the cheese mixture on top and set aside.

In a pan of water with a heatproof bowl melt the chocolate. Dip one of the sides of the leaves and set aside to cool and set. When set, peel the chocolate leaves from the rose leaves and decorate the cheesecake with them. Refigerate until set.

Serve in wedges .

Serves 6

Mango Ice Cream

Ingredients:

600ml/1 pint of milk
160g/6 oz of sugar
6 egg yolks
600ml/1 pint of cream
1 ripe mango stoned and peeled.(You can use
    1 medium tin of mangoes strained).

Method:

Bring the milk to boil in a pan.

Beat the yolks and sugar together and add to the milk. Cook the custard mixture over a low heat until thick in consistency. Do not boil.

In a blender, blend the mangoes and add to the custard mixture and mix. Place in a container, cool and freeze for 2 hours. Break up the mixture with a fork until mushy.Return to the freezer for another 2 hours. Turn into a bowl and mix the cream and freeze until firm. You can do all this in a ice cream maker instead of placing in a container to freeze.

Serves 6

Pumpkin Ice Cream

Follow the recipe above except substitute the mango for pumpkin/butternut squash.I had this in an ice cream parlour in Sarosata,Florida.

Kulfi

You can use the above recipe omitting the mangoes and substituting the cream with 1 tin of evaporated milk and adding 4-5 cinnamon pods to infuse the milk. Before freezing take out the cinnamon pods. Freeze in lolly containers or small galsses in the last freeze.

Lychee Sorbet

Ingredients:

220g/8 oz of sugar
10 lychees peeled and pitted
2 egg whites
600ml/1 pint of water

Method:

Dissolve the sugar in the water over low heat, bring to boil and boil for 2 mins.Remove from the heat.Cool.

Blitz the lychees in a blender and add to the sugar and water. Freeze in a tupaware box until the mixture is mushy.

Whisk the egg whites until stiff. Turn the mushy mixture into a bowl, fold in the egg whites and refreeze until firm. You can also do this in an ice cream maker when freezing.

Serve as a starter or dessert.

Serves 4-6

Caramelised Oranges

I had this at the Lal Quila,Bangladeshi restaurant and Chutneys vegetarian restaurant, in Drummonds Street, London in the late Eighties.

Ingredients:

8 oranges or tangerines
220g/8 oz of sugar
2 tbsp of orange liquer/essence
300ml/½ pint of water

Method:

Peel 4 of the oranges. Separate into segments. Place the orange water and cover and cook for 5 mins.until tender.

Peel the rest of the oranges and with a skewer make holes in the oranges. Place the sugar and the water in a pan,bring to boil and reduce until the sugar has caramelised. Strain the boiled oranges and place in the caramelised water. Add the essence or liquer. Cool

and place the perforated oranges in it and pour into a decorative glass bowl.Refrigerate overnight.

Serves 4

Fruit Custard

Ingredients:

1 tin of fruit cocktail or 2 bananas peeled and sliced
1 dsp of custard powder
40g/2 oz of sugar
150ml/¼ pint of milk
2 egg whites beaten into peaks

Method:

Pour the fruit in a glass bowl with the syrup.

Dissolve the custard powder in a cup with some cold milk. Heat the milk in a pan with the custard powder and the sugar. Stir continously. When it bubbles take of the heat and pour into the bowl. Cool.

Place the soft peaks of egg whites or Snow in a bowl of boiling water and let it set with the hot water.Place the Snow on top of the cooled Fruit Custard and refrigerate.

Serves 4-6

Trifle

Ingredients:

½ a Swiss roll or Maderia cake sliced
1 medium sized tin of fruit cocktail with juice
1 tbsp of sherry (optional)
½ pint of custard
1 box of jelly (optional) dissolved
Silver balls / Rainbow Sprinkle to decorate

Method:

Line the bottom and sides of a glass bowl with the cake. Pour in the fruit cocktail and if using the dissolved jelly and sherry, strain the syrup. Cool. Make the custard according to the instructions on the tin. Pour on top of the fruit and syrup. Cool and refrigerate. When set decorate with the silver balls or Rainbow Sprinkle.

Serve especially at Christmas.

Serves 6

Mousse

Ingredients:

1 box of jelly dissolved
1 medium can of evaporated milk

Method:

Mix the jelly with the milk, whisk and refrigerate until set.

Serves 6

Chocolate Mousse

Ingredients:

1 medium carton of double cream whipped
1 bar of cooking chocolate melted

Method:

Melt the chocolate in a bowl over a pan of boiling water. Mix into the whipped cream with a metal spoon. Either refrgerate in the bowl or scoop into small glasses or wine glasses and refigerate.

Serves 4

Flambe Banana

Ingredients:

1 banana peeled
1 tangerine or orange juice and zest
20g/1 oz of sugar
1 tbsp of brandy
20g/1 oz of butter melted

Method:

In the melted butter in a frying pan place the whole banana and fry for a min., turning over once. Then place the sugar and the orange juice and fry until caremalised. Pour the brandy and shake the pan until in flames. Sprinkle the zest in the pan. Take off the heat.

Serve hot in a Kidney or Banana Dish.

Serves 1

N.B. If you are non alcholic omit the brandy.

Friut Terrine

Ingredients:

40g/2 oz of mixed fresh fruits
1 box of jelly

Method:

Wash and de-stalk the fruits. Melt the jelly in boling water in a rectangle tupaware box. Place the fruits in the jelly, cover, cool and freeze until jelly is set.

When set place the box in hot water and loosen the sides of the jelly with a knife and tip upside down on a plate.

Serve in Summer.

Serves 3-4

Fresh Fruit Cake

Ingredients:

For the cake

120g/4 oz butter/margarine
80g/ 3 oz plain flour
6 eggs
220g/8 oz sugar
½ tsp of vanilla essence/2 vanilla pods

For the topping

1 medium size carton of double cream
1 kiwi,peeled and sliced
12 strawberries.hulled
2 tin peach halves
20g/1 oz of almonds chopped
½ jar of strawberry jam

Method:

Beat the butter with a whisk until soft and creamy in a bowl.

In a separate bowl place the eggs and sugar and whisk until pale and fluffy. Sift the flour into the egg and sugar mixture and fold in with a metal spoon. Fold in the the butter and vanilla essence. If using pods,split the pods in half and scrape out the paste.

Grease two 18.5cm round cake tins, flour it as well or line with grease proof paper and place the cake mixture in them. Smooth the surface with a palette knife. Bake in a oven at 180 degrees centigrade for about 40 mins. Test with a skewer, if it comes out clean it is cooked.With a knife loosen the sides, turn out on two plates by tapping the bottom of the tins. Cool on a wire rack.

Whip the double cream until doesn't fall off a metal spoon.

Melt the jam over low heat in a pan. Spread the jam on one of the sponges and sandwich together. Spread the cream on top of the gateau and the sides. Smooth with a palette knife. With a knife stick the chopped almonds on the sides of the cake.Decorate the top of the cake with the fruits, slide on to a cake platter or plate and cool in the fridge.

Serves 6-8

Pittha with Crumpets (Chittol Pittha)

Ingredients:

4-6 crumpets
600ml/1 pint of boiling milk
20-40g/2-3 oz of muscavado sugar
20g/1 oz coconut

Method:

Place the crumpets in a deep dish, sprinkle the sugar and coconut on top and then pour the boiling milk. Soak overnight in the fridge. Alternatively you can bake in the oven for 20 mins.at 190 degrees centigrade.

This can be served for breakfast as well.

Serves 4

Drinks

Kashmiri/Masala Tea

I had this at the Red Fort,Bangladeshi restaurant in Soho.

Ingredients:

1 teabag/1tsp tea leaves
A dash of milk
Sugar (optional)
1 cinammon pod
1 cinnamon bark
1 clove

Method:

Place everything in a pan. Bring to boil. Boil for 1-2 mins. Serve.

Cappuccino

Make coffee in a percolator. Boil ¼ cup of milk in the microwave, place in a cafetiere and froth,pour over the coffee.Sprinkle grated or powder chocolate on top of the cappuccino.

Latte

Follow the instruction above except boil ½ a cup milk and omit the chocolate.

Mocha

Follow the instruction for cappuccino except boil 1 cup of milk, add 1tsp of chocolate.

Spice Tea

Use the ingredients above omitting the milk and brew in a teapot.

Mango Lassi

Ingredients:

1 dsp of natural yoghurt
2 slices of mango
1 glass of milk
Sugar to taste

Method:

Place everything in a blender and blend.

Sweet Lassi

Follow the instruction above omitting the mangoes.

Melon and Mint Cocktail

Ingredients:

1 slice of water melon,pulp removed and deseeded
Sugar to taste
½ tsp of spearmint leaves
½ glass of cold water

Method:

Place everything in a blender and blend. Serve with a sprig of mint.

Pineapple and Coriander Cocktail

Follow the instruction above using 1 ring of pinneapple or some fresh pineapple with 1tsp of fresh coriander leaves.

Traditional Lemonade

Ingredients:

1 slice of lemon/lime
1 glass of cold water
Sugar to taste

Method:

Place all the ingredients in a glass and mix. You can place Spearmint leaves if you like.

Cloudy Lemonade

Use the ingredients above and add 1 egg. Blend in a blender.

Freshly Squeezed Orange Juice

Take 2 mandarins,cut in half and squeeze them in a juicer/extractor, add ½ a glass of cold water and sugar to taste and stir.

Rosewater Milk with Rose Petals

Take one glass of cold milk,add sugar to taste and 1tsp of Rose water. Decorate with fresh rose petals.

Pressed Apple Cocktail

Take 4 small apples, chop them,place in a juice extracter or blender with some water. If using a blender, sieve the juice. Add sugar to taste and some freshly ground pepper.

Raw Mango Juice

Take 2 green mangos, stone them. Chop them and place in a blender with some water,sieve it, add sugar to taste.

Srawberry or Banana Milkshake or Smoothie

Follow the above recipe except use milk instead of water. No need to sieve.

Ice Cream Punch

Take 1 scoop of Vanilla ice cream, some milk and place in a blender and blend.

Ice Cream Soda

Take a glass of cream soda and place a scoop of Vanilla ice cream on top.

Iced Tea Punch

Ingredients:

600ml/1 pint boiling water
5tsp of tea leaves or tea bags
40g/2 oz sugar
ice cubes
½ a lemon sliced
½ an orange sliced
Spearmint leaves

Meth?od:

Pour the water over the tea leaves. Brew for 2-3 mins. Strain the tea, add the sugar, lemon and orange and pour in a punch bowl. Cool. Place one box of ice cubes in the punch bowl.

Serve.

Serves 20.

Mulled Wine

Ingredients:

300ml/½ pint of water
120g/4 oz of sugar
4 cloves
1 cinnamon stick
2 lemons sliced
1 bottle of red wine
1 orange sliced

Method:

Boil the water, lemon slices and the spices for 10 mins. Add the red wine and heat gently.Pour into a punch bowl and add the orange slices.

Serve hot.

For a non-alcholic version use red grape juice instead of the wine.

Coffee Punch

Ingredients:

1 orange sliced
2 cinannamon sticks
4 cloves
Vanilla ice cream
600ml/1 pint coffee
150ml/¼ pint of brandy (optional)
Method:

Place everything except the ice cream in a punch bowl. Cool and place the Vanilla ice cream, scooped, on top floating.

Cold Coffee

Place 1 tsp of coffee, sugar to taste and some cold milk and blend in a blender.

Egg Nog

Ingredients:

1 egg
Sugar to taste
40g/2 oz of brandy/sherry(optional)
300ml/½ pint of milk

Method:

Beat the egg, add the sugar. Warm the milk and pour over the egg mixture.

Floater or Irish Coffee

Place some double cream in the freezer compartment for 15 mins. and let it thicken.

Make instant/ground coffee and pour into a glass coffee mug ¾ full. Slant the coffee mug and slowly pour in the thickened cream. It should float on top. For Irish coffee put a dash of whisky before pouring the cream.

Cranberry and Orange Fizz

Ingredients:

20g/1 oz of cranberries
1 medium size carton of fresh orange juice
1 medium size carton of cranberry juice
½ bottle of lemonade

Method:

Place everything in a punch bowl and serve.

Borhani (spicy yoghurt drink)

This is served at weddings as an appetiser as the food is very rich.
Ingredients:

300 ml of natural yoghurt
1cm of fresh ginger, peeled and grated
½ green chilli chopped
Salt to taste
½ tsp of cumin powder
Some cold water

Method:

Place everything in a blender and blend.

Colas

Take half a glass of Coke Cola and fill rest with evaporated milk and serve in Cognac Glasses. This is a nice night cap or a Christmas drink. I had this drink in Chutneys Vegetarian restaurant.

Summertime Menu

Starter *Samosa/ Onion Bhaji with Coriander Chutney*

Main Course *Chicken Biryani*

Potato Chop

Salad with a Yoghurt Dressing

or

Salmon Mousse

Salad with a French Dressing

Dessert *Faluda/Fruit Terrine*

Drinks *Alcholic-White Wine,any variety*

Non-alcholic-Soft drinks, Traditional Lemonade
Orangeade,Pineapple Juice,Apple Juice(clear or pressed)
Water Still or carbonated with Lemon slices and ice,Flavoured Water
Peach,Apricot

Post Dinner Appetiser

Pan (folded Beetle leaf),with Chun(chalk paste)chopped Beetle
Nut and Jorda(sweet,slightly intoxicating spice)

Winter Menu

Starter *Lamb Tikka served with Raita*

Main Course *Pilau rice*

Chicken Korma

Served with Mango Chutney

or

Baked Fish

Minted Potatoes

Served with Hollandaise Sauce

Dessert *Chilled Roshmalai with Chopped Almonds/Chocolate Mousse*

Drinks *Tea -Spice Tea, Earl Grey, Darjeeling, Assam, Coffee-Espresso, Mocha*

n.b. You can choose any of the drinks from the Summertime menu to drink throughout the meal.

Mouth Freshner

Mixed Sugared Masala/Mint Choccolate

Index

Printed in the United States
By Bookmasters